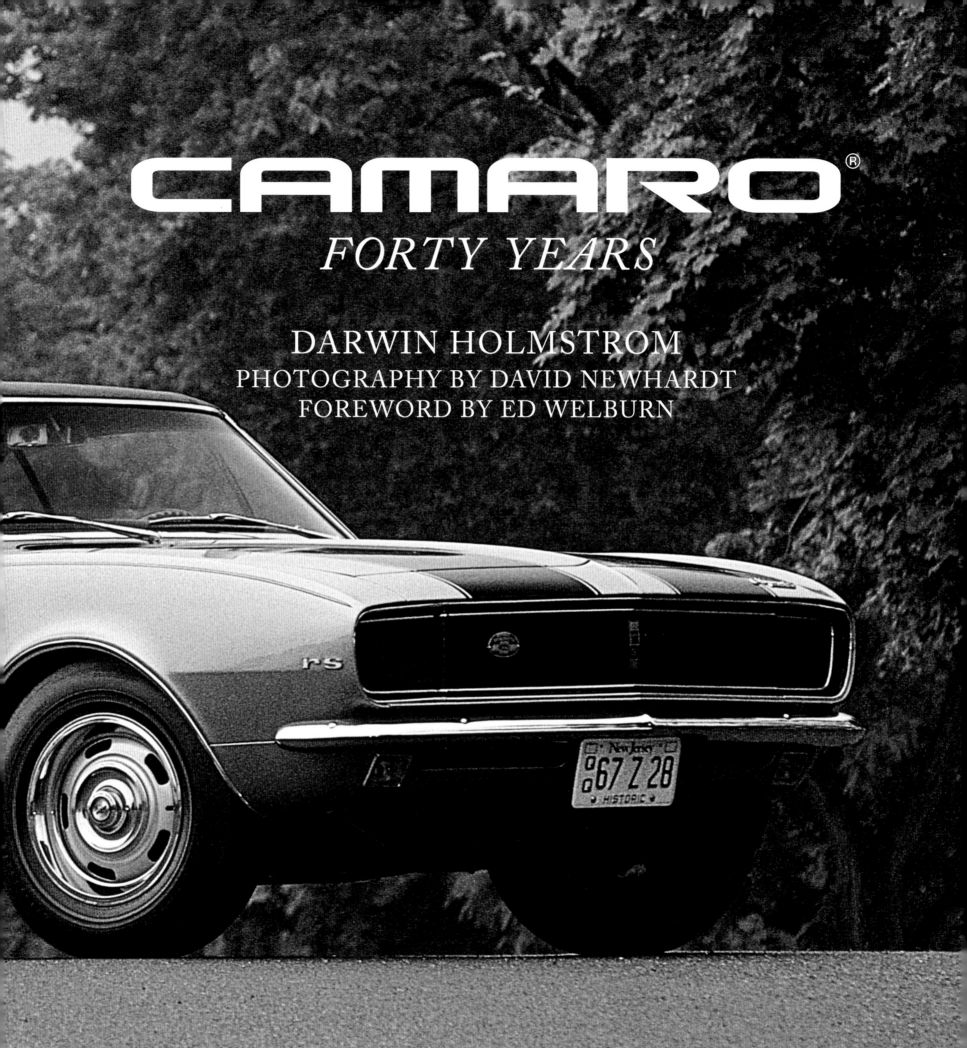

CAMARO®
FORTY YEARS

DARWIN HOLMSTROM
PHOTOGRAPHY BY DAVID NEWHARDT
FOREWORD BY ED WELBURN

First published in 2007 by Motorbooks, an imprint of MBI Publishing Company LLC, Galtier Plaza, Suite 200, 380 Jackson Street, St. Paul, MN 55101 USA

Motorbooks titles are also available at discounts in bulk quantity for industrial or sales-promotional use. For details write to Special Sales Manager at MBI Publishing Company, Galtier Plaza, Suite 200, 380 Jackson Street, St. Paul, MN 55101 USA.

To find out more about our books, join us online at www.motorbooks.com.

Library of Congress Cataloging-in-Publication Data

Holmstrom, Darwin.
  Camaro, forty years / by Darwin Holmstrom ; photography by David Newhardt ; foreword by Ed Welburn.
    p. cm.
  ISBN-13: 978-0-7603-2816-3 (hardbound w/ jacket)
  ISBN-10: 0-7603-2816-1 (hardbound w/ jacket)
  1. Camaro automobile--History. I. Newhardt, David, 1955- II. Title.
  TL215.C33H655 2007
  629.222'2--dc22

                                                    2007020951

On the cover: When Chevrolet introduced the second-generation Camaro in midyear 1970, the Z28 was once again the top performer.

On the endpaper: The fabled ZL-1 Camaros, with their all-aluminum 427-cubic-inch engines, now trade hands for upwards of $1 million apiece.

On the frontispiece: Specialty builders like Don Yenko did what General Motors would not let Chevrolet do: mount the division's biggest big-block engines in its smallest, sportiest cars.

On the title pages: When option package Z28 appeared in 1967, the only distinguishing visual characteristic was the striping on the hood and trunk lid.

On the back cover, main: When the new generation of Camaro hits the streets, this sexy convertible will be an integral part of the lineup. **Inset, top:** By 1969, Chevrolet had begun capitalizing on the killer reputation option package Z28 earned on the track and on the street by mounting Z28 badges on nearly every available surface. **Inset, middle:** The Camaro SS models built in the late 1990s and early 2000s were the fastest, best-handling Camaros built up until that time. **Inset, bottom:** The Camaro SS350 was one of the best-balanced performance cars of the muscle-car era, thanks to the lightweight-but-potent small-block V-8 under the hood.

Editor: Lindsay Hitch
Designer: Kou Lor

Printed in China

CONTENTS

FOREWORD

Cars are emotional objects. That's why books, magazines, and television shows are devoted to cars instead of dishwashers. And, as emotional objects, they leave impressions on the young and old alike.

I am pleased to write the foreword for *Camaro 40 Years* because this book celebrates the heritage of a car that has helped shape my entire life. I was in my teens when the Chevrolet Camaro was introduced, and the emotional connection was immediate. While in school, I spent my summers working at a suburban Philadelphia Chevy dealership, located roughly between Roger Penske's racing shop and the drag racing shop of Bill "Grumpy" Jenkins. I haunted these places and others, as my passion for cars was growing. It picked up even more when those first Camaros rolled off the transporter at the dealership.

No one knew it at the time, but the Camaro would go on to be a transcendent sports car—one that, because of its driving dynamics and design, attracted a diverse cross section of customers. Its image was helped by early racing success, which customers could see and *feel* in regular production models. It was also an accessible sports car and opened up a world of spirited driving to a broad audience.

Every Camaro enthusiast has his or her favorite year, engine option, or body style, and for me it was the distinctive styling of the 1969 model that epitomized the spirit of the car: great looking and fun, but also reflecting the first-generation cars' purposeful mission.

It is no stretch to say the '69 Camaro influenced my desire to design cars, and I've done just that since the day a GM designer replied to my inquiry letter about getting a start in the business, sent while I was only 11 years old. That designer's personal reply, which suggested classes to take and colleges to attend, fed the fire that was lit by my parents and still burns in me today.

Now, more than 40 years after its debut, Chevrolet is set to reintroduce the Camaro, and the timing couldn't be better. At a time when our company—and the industry itself—is facing transition, working on the Camaro has helped rally the troops. The GM Design staff worked tirelessly to perfect a design that simultaneously acknowledges the Camaro's heritage and reflects the modern design ethic at Chevrolet. My personal yellow '69 Camaro became available to the team and served as inspiration.

Not surprisingly, when word got out within the Design community at General Motors that we were working on a new Camaro design, I was flooded with unsolicited sketches from designers at many of our design centers around the globe. The final design incorporates the best ideas from a very diverse Camaro design team, with designers from not only the U.S. but Australia, Korea, and Russia.

Generations of Camaro enthusiasts will find attributes in the new Camaro that appeal to them for different reasons, and that has been our intention from the start. More than a reflection of heritage, the new Camaro underscores the recommitment at GM Design to deliver boldly designed, uncompromising automobiles. In that respect, the new Camaro is the best one ever.

Simply put, I want the new Camaro to inspire people. Who knows? It may even inspire some to become car designers.

—Ed Welburn
GM Vice President of Global Design
June 6, 2007

ACKNOWLEDGMENTS

My deepest thanks to the wonderful folks who opened their garages for this book: Jennifer Scott-Roshala, Jim Light, Louise Bent, Bill & Wanda Goldberg, Mike Steitz, Ray Sheedy, Paul Erickson, Carl Todd, Rick Hoffmeister, Mike & Linda McCusker, Rich Nielsen, Chuck Spielman, Larry Parker, David Christenholz, Cary Bongard, Charley Lillard, Michael Guarise, Richard & Elaine Bonnefoi, Leonard & Patricia Cradit, Mike and Liz Smyth, Mark Hassett, Colin Comer, and Mark Hassett Jr. Special thanks to Tammy and Gib Loudon, whose vast collection of Camaro's made the difference between success and failure. A huge thanks to Rodney W. Green at General Motors. On very short notice, he made one-of-a-kind Camaros available. A big thank you to the staff at Carlisle Events: you folks do things the way things should be done. I want to extend thanks to my publisher Motorbooks International for their continued support. I want to thank my friend and author Darwin Holmstrom for his willingness to tackle another book with me. Last but not least, I wish to thank my long-suffering wife, Susan Foxx-Newhardt, an auto widow from day one. While I'm criss-crossing the country is search of yet another Camaro, she's holding down the fort.

—David Newhardt

In addition to the people David mentioned, I'd like to thank the folks at General Motors and Equity Management, especially Scott Settlemire (the Camaro King), Ed Welburn, Matt Curran, Michael Albano, Anthony Biondo, and all the hard-working people who worked on the Camaro over the years. I'd especially like to thank our Motorbooks publishing team: Zack Miller (publisher), Lindsay Hitch (editor), and Kou Lor (designer), as well as Michael Cawcutt for his help with the cover design. In addition to being smart, hard-working, and resourceful, this is a damned fine-looking group of people.

I'd like to dedicate this book to my wife, Patricia Johnson.

—Darwin Holmstrom

INTRODUCTION
Birth of the Pony Car

On rare occasion, a car comes along that shapes its time; it defines the era in which it existed. More often than not, however, the times define the car. This is especially true of the cars built by a gigantic corporation like General Motors; an organization's willingness to take risks tends be inversely proportionate to its size, and General Motors has long been the world's largest automaker. A business organization averse to taking risks seldom produces trend-setting products. There have been exceptions—cars like Pontiac's ground-breaking GTO—but such cars have not been the rule. They've been the work of mavericks within GM's corporate bureaucracy, men like Pete Estes, Semon "Bunkie" Knudsen, John Z. DeLorean, and Vince Piggins.

In the early 1960s, General Motors' future could not have looked brighter. In fact, GM had the federal government breathing down its corporate neck for being *too* successful. The U.S. Department of Justice believed that GM was getting too large a share of the U.S. auto market. General Motors controlled nearly 57 percent of the new car market, which brought it dangerously close to violating the Sherman Antitrust Act of

What better way to impress new friends and see the nation's capital than in the all-new 1960 Chevrolet Corvair Deluxe 700 Series? Originally available as a four-door sedan, a two-door coupe became available in January 1960. *General Motors Corp. Used with permission, GM Media Archives*

A performance enthusiast, Semon "Bunkie" Knudsen injected excitement into ailing Pontiac during the 1950s. Due to his success at Pontiac, he was promoted to head Chevrolet in 1961. In 1965, he was elevated to vice president. *General Motors Corp. Used with permission, GM Media Archives*

1890, the antitrust law designed to prevent one company from monopolizing an entire industry. The Department of Justice warned GM that if it ever got to 60 percent of the market, it would break up the company just as it had done earlier in the century with Standard Oil.

But the auto industry is a volatile business, and by the mid-1960s, a small car from rival Ford Motor Company had astute members of GM management genuinely worried. That car was the Mustang. Not only was the car selling in unheard-of numbers, it was selling to the market that everyone wanted to tap: the baby boomers.

Elliot Marantette "Pete" Estes oversaw the successful introduction of the Oldsmobile Rocket V-8 engine in the 1950s. He succeeded Bunkie Knudsen as president of Chevrolet Division in 1965, where he kept the emphasis on performance across the entire product line. *General Motors Corp. Used with permission, GM Media Archives*

Between the years 1946 and 1964, Americans had approximately 76 million children. By 1962, this population had begun to earn drivers' licenses. By the middle of the decade, they were graduating from high school, getting jobs, and buying lots and lots of cars. Every automaker in America, with the possible exception of poor, clueless American Motors, coveted the baby-boom market. It didn't take Nostradamus to see the profit potential in exploiting this huge population explosion.

In the early years of the decade, the corporate management at Chrysler, GM, and Ford didn't quite understand how to capitalize on this market. For the most part, they

Chevrolet's Corvair, introduced in 1960, quickly garnered accolades from the popular press, including "Car of the Year" honors from *Motor Trend*. While the opposed six-cylinder engine didn't rival a hydroelectric plant for power, its 80 horsepower pushed the Corvair along at a tidy clip. *General Motors Corp. Used with permission, GM Media Archives*

continued to produce the same family-friendly sedans they had always produced, but as this vast swell of young people entered the market, it became clear that the same old, same old held limited appeal for a new generation with new tastes.

This new breed of auto buyer wanted power, a commodity that America's V-8-powered cars produced in abundance, but the young consumers entering the auto market in the mid-1960s wanted more than just power. They wanted style. They wanted cars that turned heads when they cruised down the Main Streets of America's towns and cities. They wanted cars that did not look like their parents' cars, the cars in which Detroit manufacturers mounted their powerful V-8 engines. They wanted smaller, sportier cars.

Smaller, Sportier, Sexier

For the most part, the committees designing cars for the American auto industry seemed to be staffed by members who failed to grasp the demands of young buyers, but a few savvy marketers in the U.S. auto industry understood that they could exploit the desires of the baby-boom generation to sell cars.

John Zachary DeLorean was controversial even during his tenure at General Motors. He started his career at Chrysler, and then went to Packard. With the collapse of Packard, he went to GM, where he worked his way up to the head of Pontiac at age 40. In February 1969, he was tapped to lead Chevrolet. *General Motors Corp. Used with permission, GM Media Archives*

Ford was the first major U.S. automaker to develop a new small car for the 1960s. On October 8, 1959, Ford introduced the Falcon, a shrunken version of its larger sedans. A thoroughly conventional and uninspiring 144-cubic-inch inline six-cylinder engine powered the Falcon, but the little car broke new technological ground by using unitized-body construction, which incorporated an integrated frame and body instead of placing a separate body on top of a ladder-type frame

The Falcon sold extremely well and earned a profit for Ford, but it failed to ignite the passion of younger buyers. The only way the Falcon could be less sexy would have been if it had been renamed the "Carbuncle." Ford achieved record sales with the Falcon, but the car was not a hit with the kids.

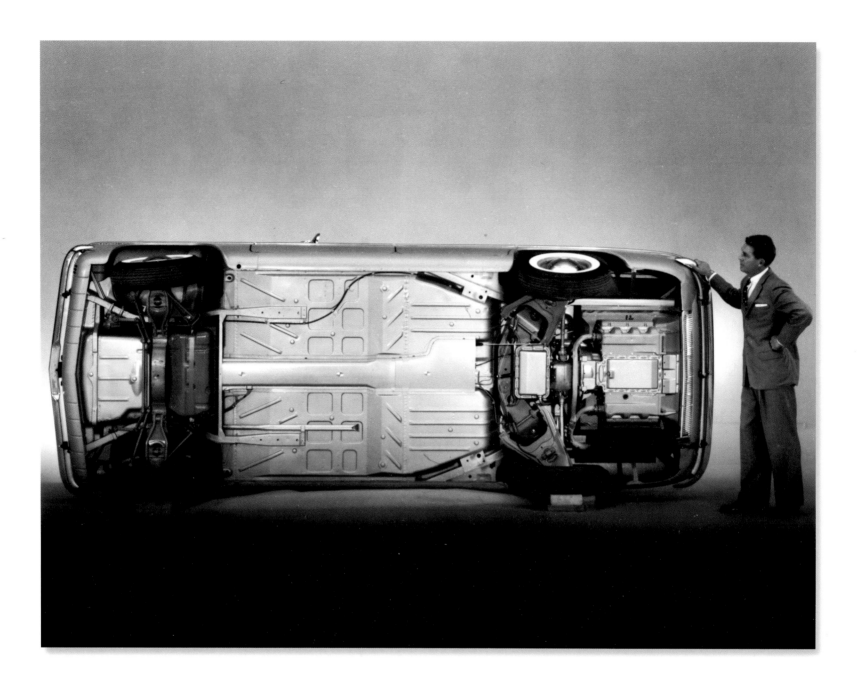

With a 1960 Corvair tipped on its side, it's easy to see the fully independent suspension. When it debuted, the rear suspension utilized swing axles and lacked a rear anti-sway bar, the primary reasons that Ralph Nader lambasted the vehicle in his book, *Unsafe at Any Speed*. *General Motors Corp. Used with permission, GM Media Archives*

Now for Something Completely Different

Chevrolet took a completely different approach when it introduced its new small car for the 1960 model year, offering a compact that used technology never before seen on an American-made automobile. Like Ford, Chevrolet had the smaller part of the smaller, sexier equation mastered; standing only 51.3 inches tall and measuring just 66.9 inches wide, the Corvair took up less garage space than any other car rolling out of Detroit at that time.

The Corvair was the smallest American-made car of its day, and it was also the most technologically different. Its engine—an air-cooled opposed six-cylinder—sat in the rear of the car, where it drove the rear wheels through a transaxle transmission.

The Corvair's drivetrain layout may not have followed the pattern set by other cars from Detroit, but when compared to the cars being imported from Europe, it seemed less strange. The Corvair used technology very similar to the German-built Volkswagen Beetle, the most popular import of the period. The Beetle featured the same rear-mounted, air-cooled engine design as the Corvair. In 1960, Volkswagen sold nearly 160,000 of its odd little sedans.

The Corvair sold well enough in its first year—250,000 units—but compared to the nearly half-million Falcons Ford sold in 1960, it could hardly be considered a sales success.

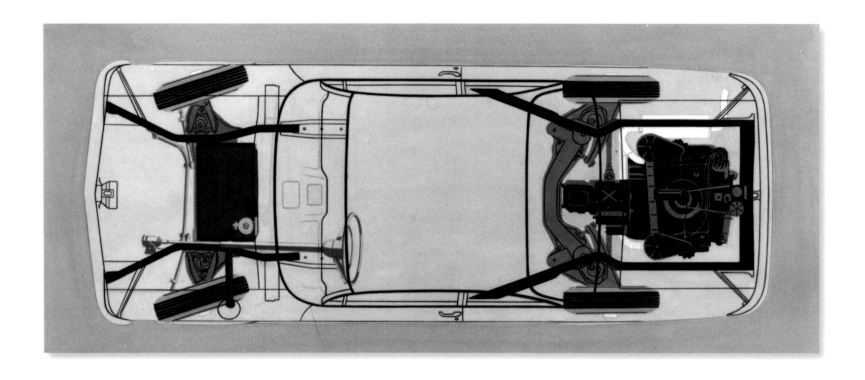

This illustration of the 1962 Corvair Sport Club Coupe shows the front and rear suspension subframes attaching to the unibody structure. Note the distance the engine was set behind the rear wheels; under severe handling, the engine mass could act like a pendulum and compromise vehicle control. *General Motors Corp. Used with permission, GM Media Archives*

Chevy Small Car, Take II

Chevrolet's designers realized the Corvair used too much new technology for the comfort of many American buyers. The Chevy II, introduced in September of 1961, used unitized-body construction, but otherwise it was a very conventional design.

Chevrolet marketers tried to inject a bit of excitement into the new Chevy II in an attempt to appeal to the youth market and created the Nova 400. This car did nothing to appease the growing demand for more powerful cars, since its 194-cubic-inch inline six produced a mere 120 horsepower, enough to give the sub-2,600-pound coupe adequate acceleration but not enough to impress buyers lusting after the performance offered by Detroit's big V-8 sedans. The Chevy II sold better than the Corvair—Chevy dealers moved 325,000 units for 1962—but not well enough to outsell the Falcon.

Chevrolet took its Corvair in a sportier direction in its sophomore year in an attempt to fill its coffers with more youth-market dollars. By adding bucket seats and a four-speed transmission as standard equipment, Chevrolet designers created the sporty Corvair Monza. Falcon sales rose during the car's second year on the market, but not at the rate Corvair sales rose. Falcons still outsold Corvairs nearly two-to-one, but thanks to the appeal of the sporty Monza, the littlest Chevy had closed the gap at a rapid pace in just one year.

Sexing the Falcon

In response to the success of the sexier Corvair, Ford sexed up its Falcon, creating the Falcon Futura. Like the Monza, the Futura featured bucket seats and a four-speed transmission, prerequisites for a sporty car. Powering the Futura was a tarted-up

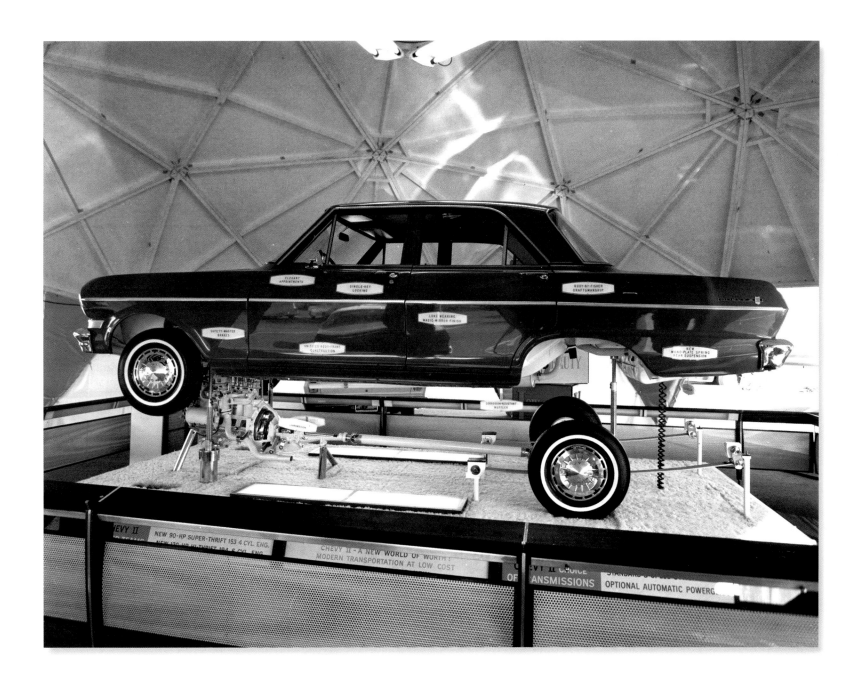

170-cubic-inch inline six that generated 101 horsepower—quite a few more than the standard 144-cubic-inch engine, but it was still a six.

To attract the growing number of young buyers, the new breed of small cars coming from Detroit needed V-8 power. Ford understood this, and in 1963 unveiled the Sprint version of the Falcon Futura. The Sprint featured Ford's newly developed small-block V-8 that used advanced thin-wall casting techniques, resulting in a lightweight powerplant perfectly suited for installation in a compact car like the Falcon.

Chevrolet responded with a sporty SS package for the Nova, which featured special trim, bucket seats, and enhanced instrumentation, but still no V-8. The original Nova SS retained Chevy's unsporting inline six.

In order to let the public see that there was no air-cooled engine lurking in the 1962 Chevy II 300's rear trunk, a "lift" car was built. Note the long rear leaf springs attached to the rear live axle; this was a cost-effective solution for creating a comfortable ride with minimal expense. *General Motors Corp. Used with permission, GM Media Archives*

Chevrolet's Falcon fighter, the Chevy II, debuted in 1962. Devoid of expensive options, the economical Chevy II boasted four- and six-cylinder engines. However, a dealer-installed factory option allowed for the fitting of either a 283-ci or 327-ci V-8 with their attendant tire-melting power. *General Motors Corp. Used with permission, GM Media Archives*

In 1964, the Chevy II finally got a V-8. Although not a fire-breather, the two-barrel 283-cubic-inch small-block V-8 in the Chevy II produced 195 horsepower, enough to propel the diminutive Chevrolet through the quarter-mile traps in 18 seconds.

While the new V-8 was enough to push the Chevy II through the quarter-mile in a respectable time, it wasn't enough to push it ahead of the competition in the marketplace. Chevy II sales fell 48 percent in 1964. The slow sales may have been due in part to a lack of style, power, or speed, but a greater factor was the stiff competition for baby-boomer dollars. One particular car Ford introduced as a mid-1964 model was giving Chevrolet dealers epileptic fits.

Mustang Mania

Ford Division General Manager Lido "Lee" Iacocca understood the importance of cracking the youth market. Iacocca had pondered the sales potential of an attractively styled Falcon since the car's introduction. Not that the Falcon needed help; the car's first-year Falcon sales of 417,174 units set a sales record for an American manufacturer.

But, as always happens, the market changed. The new sportier cars from Chevrolet—the Corvair Monza and the Nova SS—began to bite into Falcon sales and erode Ford's share of the compact-car market.

When Iacocca was promoted to vice president and general manager of Ford Division, he formed the Fairlane Committee, a team assigned to brainstorm ideas for Ford's future direction. The Falcon Futura was one of the first products of the Fairlane Committee.

The Futura Sprint proved to be one of the pivotal cars of the era, not because it was the most exciting vehicle on the market—it was far from that—but because it formed the basic platform of one of the most exciting vehicles ever produced, the car that in many ways defined the entire baby-boom generation: the Mustang.

Targeted at the young family, the 1962 Chevy II 300 Series was a sensible alternative to the Ford Falcon. Spare, clean lines would be a Chevy II hallmark throughout the 1960s. Chevrolet used the Chevy II as the entry-level vehicle in its product lineup. The Chevy II brought first-time buyers into Chevrolet showrooms. *General Motors Corp. Used with permission, GM Media Archives*

Iacocca encouraged his designers to go one step beyond the Futura Sprint and develop a sporty four-seat car. This "special Falcon," a two-plus-two-seat car (a car with minimal rear seats) based on the Falcon chassis, was to cost no more than $2,500 and weigh no more than 2,500 pounds.

The resulting Mustang sold so well that it completely changed the relationship between baby boomers and the auto industry. Ford introduced the Mustang as a 1964 1/2 model on April 17, 1964. By the end of that day, Ford had sold over 22,000 Mustangs. By year's end, it had sold 263,434 units, and by the end of the Mustang's first full year on the market, Ford had sold 418,812 of the sporty machines, breaking the record set just a few years earlier by the Falcon.

In its most basic form, the Mustang represented little more than a Falcon with pretty sheet metal. In addition to its chassis, it shared the Falcon's standard 170-cubic-inch, 101-horsepower inline six. Where the Falcon and the Mustang parted ways was in the shape of the sheet metal. The Mustang's short trunk, long hood, and aggressive stance shared none of the Falcon's meek economy-car profile. When outfitted with one of the optional V-8 engines, available from the outset, the Mustang had the beans to back up its good looks. The top-of-the-line, 210-horsepower, 289-cubic-inch D-code engine made the Mustang one of the quickest mass-produced cars this side of a GTO.

With the Mustang, Ford had not just developed the perfect automobile for the emerging baby-boom market; it had developed the perfect automotive genre for baby boomers: the pony car.

When Ford introduced the Mustang, it created an entirely new breed of car, one perfectly suited for the emerging baby boom market.

CHAPTER ONE

GENERAL MOTORS REACTS

The year 1968 marked the first year that ventless side windows were incorporated, due to the introduction of Astro Ventilation. The result was a cleaner Daylight Opening (DLO).

Ford couldn't credit its success in tapping the youth market to any lack of effort on the part of Chevrolet. Between the Corvair Monza, the Chevy II Nova, the Chevelle SS, the Corvette, and the Impala SS, Chevrolet offered a comprehensive line of from which baby boomers could choose. While all those cars had their fans and experienced varying degrees of success, none triggered the baby boomers' buy impulse the way the Mustang did.

Initially, Chevrolet responded to the Mustang by doing what had worked in 1961—building a sexier version of the Corvair. The restyled 1965 Corvair could be ordered with a state-of-the-art turbocharger, giving it impressive acceleration for a six, but it was still a six, and a darned odd one at that. To make matters worse, it had become a target for self-righteous crusaders hell-bent on saving young people from their lust for sporty cars.

Some people within the GM understood that Chevy's offerings, good as they were, would not be enough to attract the growing number of young buyers. A few visionaries

Above: Side marker lights made their debut on the 1968 model vehicles, including the Camaro SS. The grille was simple yet aggressive, and the contrasting SS nose stripe offered a great visual counterpoint.

Left: With the bias-ply tires used on performance vehicles like the 1967 Camaro, heavily bolstered seats were not really needed; cornering g-forces were relatively low due to the lack of lateral grip.

It's August 1962, and dapper William Mitchell, GM design czar, is showing Irv Rybicki and staff his design proposals for the 1963 Corvette. Mitchell prided himself on his appearance, whether it was in the office, behind the wheel, or on one of his sport motorcycles. *General Motors Corp. Used with permission, GM Media Archives*

had been even begun working on a sporty car for the youth market before the Mustang blew that market wide open.

The Mini Riv'

General Motors' design studio, headed by Design Vice President Bill Mitchell, introduced the Buick Riviera for the 1963 model year in an attempt to compete with Ford's popular four-seat Thunderbird. The car proved extremely popular, and Chevrolet's Chief Designer, Irv Rybicki, thought a smaller, less-expensive Chevrolet interpretation of the sporty-coupe concept pioneered by the Riviera would be a good addition to Chevrolet's lineup. With Mitchell's support, he secretly began working on such a car in 1962.

Irv Rybicki, group chief designer at Chevrolet design during the Camaro's gestation, succeeded Bill Mitchell as head of GM design staff in 1977 after Mitchell resigned. He served in that capacity until 1986, when he was replaced by Chuck Jordan. *General Motors Corp. Used with permission, GM Media Archives*

Like the Mustang, the car used the underpinnings of an economy car as a starting point—in this case, Chevrolet's recently introduced Chevy II economy sedan. Rybicki's concept car followed the Mustang's pony car design formula: a short rear deck and a long hood. The resulting clay mockup bore a remarkable resemblance to Ford's upcoming Mustang, though any similarities were unintentional; Mitchell and Rybicki didn't even know about Ford's upcoming pony car.

Chevrolet Division Manager Bunkie Knudsen liked the concept car but worried that it would cannibalize sales from other models, particularly the Corvair and the Chevy II. Worse yet for the sporty Chevy design study, Chevrolet planned to introduce the Chevelle, its version of the intermediate A-body chassis. Knudsen worried that

Henry "Hank" Haga headed Chevrolet Design Studio 2, which handled the design of what would be the 1967 Camaro. The first-generation Camaro can trace some of its design cues to the 1965 Corvair. *General Motors Corp. Used with permission, GM Media Archives*

adding another sporty model to the mix would only slice the same amount of pie into increasingly smaller pieces.

The Super Nova

Late the following year, Hank Haga, chief of Chevrolet's Design Studio 2, developed a similar concept: the Super Nova. Mitchell and retired Design Vice President Harley Earl liked the car enough to develop a running prototype for the show car circuit. The public reacted well to the new car when it debuted at the World's Fair in New York in early 1964, but GM's upper management was less enthusiastic. They wanted to maximize return on the money the company had invested developing the Corvair and rightly feared that a car like the one Haga developed would kill Corvair sales. Had the automotive status quo that existed at the time the Super Nova made its debut remained the same, this decision might have been wise. But just a few weeks after GM displayed the Super Nova, Ford revolutionized the auto industry by introducing the new Mustang.

Some folks within GM management failed to realize that with the introduction of a single model, Ford had revolutionized the business of selling automobiles in America. They completely underestimated Ford's new pony car, judging the Mustang's boxy styling and flat body panels as old-fashioned and unappealing. In his book *Camaro*, author Gary Witzenburg, a young engineering student interning at Chevrolet at the time Ford introduced the Mustang, describes Mitchell's response to the question: "When will Chevy have an answer to the Mustang?"

"We already have," Mitchell bellowed. "It's called the Corvair."

The fact that GM ignored the Mustang at first can in part be blamed on GM's corporate structure, which kept top executives isolated from the realities of the marketplace; they genuinely didn't know that Ford was selling Mustangs faster than it could build them. They had been misinformed that the Mustang wasn't selling well, so when they learned that Ford had sold more than 100,000 Mustangs in two months, it shook the hidebound corporation to its very core.

GM Awakens

The Mustang's sales numbers provided GM management with a much-needed slap in the face, forcing them to face the new marketplace realities. GM would have to accept that the Corvair could never be a player in this new pony car game and develop a Chevrolet answer to Ford's Mustang.

Once again a core group of enthusiasts within Chevrolet came to the rescue. These men understood the urgency with which the division needed to enter the burgeoning pony car market. This group included Mitchell, himself; though he had publicly proclaimed the Corvair a competitor, he was just putting the best possible face on a dismal situation. Privately, he knew that the only way to compete with Ford was to field a car similar to the concepts that Rybicki and Haga had developed, though he wasn't ready to abandon the Corvair technology; behind the scenes he continued to champion a high-performance version of the Corvair.

Chevrolet's entry into the pony car market would need to be a spectacular car, better than the Mustang in every measure. Given that the Mustang would have more than two years to develop a market and a reputation on the street, the new Chevy would have to be sportier, more comfortable, better looking, and most importantly, better performing. It would have to be quicker in a quarter-mile, have a faster top-end speed, and handle better than the Ford. And it would have to utilize the Mustang's conventional design, with a liquid-cooled engine in front driving the rear wheels. This meant that Chevy's new pony car, internally coded the "F" body project (often theorized

Shown is the 1962 Chevrolet Chevy II front unitized structure, utilizing a subframe assembly bolted to the cowl. Chevrolet engineers found that the first-generation Chevy II suffered from uncomplimentary driving characteristics and insufficient noise, vibration, and harshness (NVH) isolation. *General Motors Corp. Used with permission, GM Media Archives*

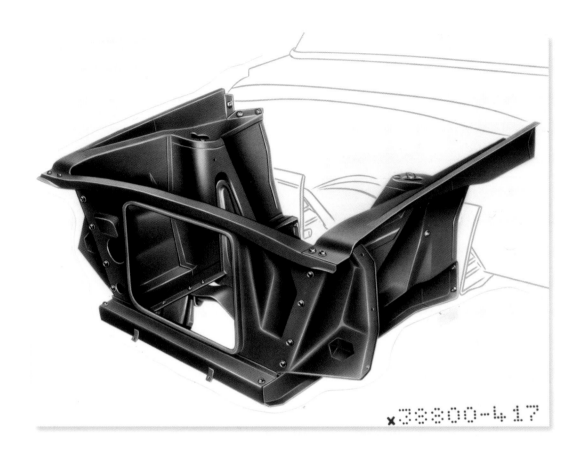

The attached bodywork added rigidity to the Chevy II's subframe structure. *General Motors Corp. Used with permission, GM Media Archives*

Ed Cole was general manager of Chevrolet when he posed with a 1960 Corvair Deluxe 700 Series four-door sedan. A real car guy, he was responsible for the famous small-block V-8 in 1955 and was a proponent of the diminutive rear-drive Corvair. He retired from General Motors in 1974 as president of the corporation. *General Motors Corp. Used with permission, GM Media Archives*

to be an allusion to the obvious fact that it had come into existence as a direct response to Ford's popular pony car, though in reality it was simply a random letter assigned to the car), would utilize architecture similar to Rybicki's and Haga's earlier sporty coupe concept cars rather than be a version of Mitchell's super Corvair idea.

Fast-Track Fast Car

Because of GM's tardiness in fielding an entry into the pony car market, designers and engineers didn't have much time to develop a competitor for the Mustang. One of the most efficient ways to bring a car to market in the shortest possible time is to use parts-bin engineering and develop a car based on as many existing components as possible. Like Rybicki's clay mockup and Haga's Super Nova show car, the new Chevy pony car would be based on the existing Chevy II economy car chassis. This was fitting, since it is exactly what Ford had done when it based its sporty Mustang on the lowly Falcon chassis.

Taut styling set the 1967 Camaro apart from the pony car crowd, while an option list a mile long allowed buyers to tailor the vehicles according to their taste and budget. While the powerful V-8 engines got the press, the $2,466 six-cylinder Camaro sport coupe was what a lot of customers put into their garages. Note that this example features 1968 wheel covers.

Engine-displacement badging on the front fenders let the world know what kind of power a 1967 Camaro was packing. A "250" on the bodywork meant that a 250-cubic-inch straight-six engine was handling propulsion chores. Standard rolling stock on this model Camaro consisted of 7.3x14 bias-ply tires, well suited for containing the six-cylinder's modest power.

Given that the new car would be based on the economy-oriented Chevy II platform, making a world-class sporty car would be a tall order for Chevrolet's engineers and designers. The Chevy II had been designed to be economical; it was not designed to possess breathtaking acceleration, stellar handling, or a quiet, comfortable ride.

But Chevy engineers had more freedom to develop the chassis for the new sport coupe than Ford engineers had been given when creating the Mustang from the Falcon, because the Chevy II platform was scheduled for a redesign for the 1968 model year. This meant that the division could utilize the money and effort spent designing the new Mustang-beater when it developed the new Chevy II, thereby amortizing development costs much more quickly. Because of this, Chevy engineers were able to develop a much-improved unit-body chassis for their new pony car.

Digital Design

Sharing development with the new Chevy II may have given Chevrolet's development team some breathing room in the budget, but it didn't do anything to resolve the condensed development schedule needed to get the car to market in time to take a bite out of Mustang sales. Engineers could do pretty much what they needed to do, but they had to do it quickly. To help speed up development, engineers utilized new computer technology to help design the car. The F cars and second-generation Chevy II

Not every buyer needed a V-8 to get the new 1967 Camaro down the road; many chose the optional 250-cubic-inch, straight six-cylinder engine. This reliable powerplant generated 155 horsepower and cost a whopping $26.35 over the standard 230-ci engine.

Not every Camaro was equipped with a sporty floor shifter. A few of the thrifty six-cylinder models used a column shifter.

Riding on a 108.1-inch wheelbase, the 1967 Camaro sport coupe exhibited lithe, spare styling. The name Camaro was a last-minute choice. The name was selected at the point when tooling for the badges had to be made.

were first the first cars to rely on computers for calculating chassis dimensions, calibrating suspension settings, and producing prototype parts. In its December 1966 issue, *Road & Track* wrote:

> In the search for an aerodynamically sound style, Chevrolet enlisted the aid of a computer. The computer didn't exactly design the car, but it quickly affirmed or denied the progressing work. A few clicks, buzzes and flashing lights—the computer arrived at a final answer on how the Camaro should ride.

This was pretty heady stuff at the time; never mind that the computers in question possessed a fraction of the power of today's garden-variety Blackberry.

The new Chevy needed to be in dealer showrooms as soon as possible to capture some of the Mustang's record-breaking sales. In addition to making use of computers to an unprecedented extent, Chevrolet engineers put in a lot of overtime.

The solid-axle rear suspension was sourced from the Chevy II, complete with single leaf springs. With unibody construction from the cowl back, the rear suspension bolted directly to the structure.

A Better Nova

Chevy's chassis engineers focused their efforts on the connection between the front subframe (Chevrolet referred to it as a "stub frame") of the Chevy II and the main body, the weakest link in the original Chevy II design. In a way, the Chevy II was a hybrid between a traditional body-on-frame chassis and a modern unit-body chassis. From the cowl rearward, the car used unit-body construction, but the engine and front suspension were attached to a separate subframe that was more like a traditional ladder-frame design. The subframe bolted to the main chassis at the cowl, effectively making the chassis a two-piece structure.

In the original Chevy II design, the subframe ended at the cowl and was solidly bolted to the main body. This created a zone of flex in the chassis, leading to awkward handling, and it also transmitted an unacceptable amount of vibration into the passenger compartment.

When Ford introduced the Mustang in April 1964, it offered a sporty version. Chevrolet went one better when it released the 1967 Camaro RS, an optional appearance package unlike any option Ford offered for the Mustang.

Flat seat cushions did little to hold occupants in place, but the interior of the 1967 Camaro RS was a handsome place. The steering wheel hinted at its Corvette cousin.

To eliminate flex, Chevy's chassis engineers extended the members of the subframe back past the cowl under the floorpan all the way to the front-seat area. The front clip—the sheet metal attached to the subframe—also contributed to the car's overall rigidity. These changes combined to give the car the stiff chassis that a sporty coupe would need to handle as well as, or preferably better than, a Mustang. To give the F car a smoother, quieter ride, Chevrolet used four tuned double-biscuit rubber mounts between the subframe and passenger compartment to eliminate noise and vibration. The result was a chassis that was sportier and more luxurious than the Chevy II. More importantly, it was sportier and more luxurious than the Falcon-based Mustang.

Chevy designers also modified the suspension extensively. To beat the popular Mustang, the F car would need a suspension that was considerably more sophisticated than the relatively crude arrangement on the Chevy II. While far from state-of-the-art, the front suspension of the F car, which featured short upper and wide lower control arms, with coil springs mounted to the lower control arms and a structural

Many Camaro RSs were fitted with the optional RPO L30 engine. Displacing 327 cubic inches, it was rated at 275 horsepower and cost $92.70: a bargain. Beneath the air cleaner was a four-barrel carburetor.

suspension crossmember tying the whole thing together, was sophisticated enough to provide good handling, especially with the 0.687-inch front anti-sway bar that all versions of the F car received.

Standard brakes were conventional 9.5-inch drums at all four corners, but 11-inch disc brakes were optional up front. The base disc setup would set a buyer back $79, and the power-assisted versions cost an additional $42. If the buyer wanted to spend an additional $37, he or she could opt for metallic-lined rear brake shoes, a worthy upgrade.

By the time the F-body design was finalized, time was running short and the car's rear suspension was more or less lifted directly from the Chevy II. This setup, which featured a solid rear axle suspended on single-leaf springs, would prove to be the weakest part of the new F-car chassis design. Cars equipped with V-8 engines and four-speed transmissions used a single radius rod on the right side of the rear axle to help tame rear axle hop, but more help would be needed to bring the blue-light-special rear suspension up to the standards set by the rest of the car.

In its production form, the new F body would have a 108-inch wheelbase and measure 184.7 inches long, 1.5 inches longer than the Chevy II.

Topless F Body

Fairly late in the development of the new F body, Chevy's testers discovered that because of its more flexible chassis, the convertible version of the car exhibited cyclic oscillations so severe that, if they weren't counteracted, the car would shake itself to pieces.

The graceful lines of the full-width grille were maintained on RPO Z22 Rally Sport Camaros by using electrically activated doors in front of the headlights. Chevrolet priced the Rally Sport option at $105.35.

Engineers tried all the usual tricks to stiffen the convertible's chassis, such as adding structural members behind the rocker panels, stiffening the underbody, reinforcing the windshield pillars, and even adding heavy strikers to the doors, but nothing worked. They finally resorted to harmonic balancers (known as "cocktail shakers") at all four corners of the car. These oil-filled cylinders contained spring-suspended weights at each corner. They added nearly 70 pounds of weight to the car, but they took care of the oscillation problem.

High Style

If the rear suspension was the car's weakest link, the styling would prove to be its strongest selling point—the aspect of the car that would turn the F body from a Mustang wanna-be into an icon in its own right.

Hank Haga's studio received the assignment to develop the new F car, which was to be based on Rybicki's design study. With the help of Assistant Studio Chief John Schinella, Haga's crew quickly developed a clay concept. The smooth, organic curves of Italian cars influenced Haga, and the design his studio produced was much rounder and more flowing than the crisp, sharp-edged Mustang. Like the revised A-body cars GM introduced in 1966, the new F body featured graceful arcs over the wheelwells, a shape that earned the nickname "Coke bottle design" because the cars resembled bottles of Coca-Cola laid on their sides.

While the new car would feature design cues from GM's popular A bodies, designers went out of their way to avoid making the new F body resemble the Corvair. The Corvair was rapidly falling out of favor in the marketplace after the publication of Ralph Nader's *Unsafe at Any Speed*, a book-length diatribe against the Corvair. Nader had legitimate complaints about the overall safety of all cars in the mid-1960s—the safety technology of the period was crude, at best—but singling out the Corvair was

unfair and uninformed. The original Corvair needed some suspension tweaking, and it was hypersensitive to maintaining proper tire pressure, but when properly set up and maintained, it was roughly as safe as other compact cars on the market. When Nader demonized that particular model, he killed it in the marketplace, and Chevrolet did not want its ncw pony car taintcd by association.

The interior of the Camaro had the pizzazz to match the stylish exterior. The Camaro interior came in two trim levels: Base and Custom. Like the Corvair Monza, bucket seats were standard, though a bench seat was available as an extra-cost option. Few buyers seemed willing to pay for this feature, though quite a few buyers saw the value in spending $26.35 for the fold-down rear bench seat.

The Custom interior featured seat material and door panels with different patterns, a molded trunk mat, glove compartment lighting, extra sound-deadening insulation, and a special steering wheel. For an additional $31.60, a buyer could order a walnut-grained steering wheel, and for another $42.15, he or she could have that wheel mounted to a Comfortilt steering column. An especially desirable interior option available

Camaro's introductory year, 1967, was the only model year that used side vent windows. Starting in 1968, Astro Ventilation was introduced, eliminating the need for the vent windows.

When the Camaro originally debuted on September 12, 1966, the top model was the SS350. The RS appearance package, which featured covered headlights, could be added to any Camaro, up to and including the SS350.

Model year 1967 was the only year that V-8 Camaros had both rear shock absorbers mounted in front of the live axle. Future years would see a staggered configuration to help minimize axle hop under hard acceleration.

on V-8-powered cars, coded U17, mounted the fuel, oil, battery, and temperature gauges and a clock in pods on a console around the floor-mounted shift lever. The option sheet for the Camaro was so inclusive that money was really the only limiting factor when creating a truly luxurious pony car.

Overlapping Pistons

The F body broke little new ground in the engine bay, but the Mustang hadn't either, and the lack of engine innovation hadn't hampered Mustang sales. For the most part, engine choices came from Chevrolet's existing stable of powerplants, ranging from a 230-cubic-inch inline six that generated 140 horsepower to a 275-horsepower 327-cubic-inch V-8. Only one engine—the 350-cubic-inch small-block V-8—was unique to the new Chevy.

General Motors Group Vice President Ed Cole, who had overseen the development of original Chevy small-block V-8 when he was the general manager of Chevrolet a decade earlier, personally ordered Donald H. McPherson, Chevrolet's chief engineer for passenger cars, to bore out the 327 and create a 350-cubic-inch version of the venerable small-block. Unfortunately, the basic architecture of the block precluded such overboring. In his book *Camaro*, Witzenburg quotes McPherson's response to Cole's directive:

"Cole came along one day," McPherson remembers, "and got a hold of me and said, 'I want to go to 350 cubic inches, and I want it all in bore.' It took me a month and a half to collar him and show him a layout proving it was pretty tough to have the pistons overlap one another. I said, 'Where do you want me to put the flat spots on the rings?'"

Unable to have the pistons of the new 350 overlap one another, McPherson had to resort to increasing piston stroke, which created a number of additional challenges for his team of engineers. A longer stroke leads to higher peak piston speeds at a given rpm. A piston traveling up and down along a 3.48-inch stroke 3,000 times each minute is moving a lot faster than a piston traveling along a 3.25-inch stroke 3,000 times during that same amount of time. Increased piston speeds lead to all kinds of engineering challenges—challenges McPherson and his team worked long hours to overcome.

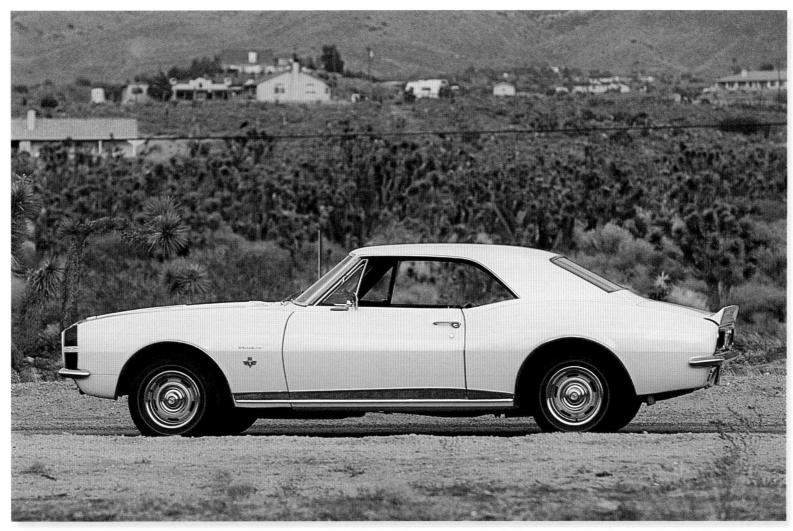

General Motors' stylists incorporated a Coke-bottle design on the 1967 Camaro. This pinching of the waist reduced the visual mass between the wheels while adding drama to the lines.

The 1967 Camaro rode on a 108-inch wheelbase, exactly matching its Mustang competition. Coupes were 51 inches tall and had a width of 72.5 inches, about 1.5 inches wider that the Mustang.

From its debut year, the Camaro SS could be teamed with the Rally Sport option to create a visually arresting automobile. The bumblebee nose stripe was part of the Super Sport option.

Because McPherson's engine would appear in the top-of-the-line F body, in high-output 295-horse form, McPherson's assignment bordered on impossible. Impossible, but necessary. By 1965, as F-body development was running at top speed, U.S. auto buyers had developed a seemingly insatiable appetite for more and more power. A Nova-like SS trim package overlaid on a car powered by the same old pedestrian engines would no longer cut it.

Putting the Car before the Name

In 1966, before an official name had been chosen for the car, Chevrolet presented a fleet of 20 cars to the press. The press and public had already taken to calling the upcoming Chevrolet the "Panther," though internally it was still called the F body. This fleet of cars marked the beginning of an unprecedented public relations blitz that led up to the official unveiling of Chevy's new pony car on September 12 of that year. The blitz worked, and the press and public were in a frothy lather by the time the new Chevy hit the streets.

Developed for the track-oriented Z28 option, the tail spoiler was available on non-Z28 Camaros as well, imparting a heavy dose of sport onto any vehicle to which it was fitted.

The name "Panther" was used within the halls of General Motors as well as in the press, though other names were hinted at. In the April 8, 1965, issue of *Detroit News*, reporter Jack Crellin mentioned "Colt" and "Chevette" as possible names for Chevy's upcoming pony car. The name "Panther" certainly sounded like something that could turn a Mustang into a tasty snack, but GM's corporate stress puppies, still stinging from Nader's crusade against the Corvair, worried that the name would sound too aggressive and anger the safety Nazis.

One concept—"Gemini"—played off the corporate initials "GM," but just as regular production was about to begin, Chevrolet decided to continue with the tradition of giving cars names that started with the letter C: "Corvette," "Corvair," "Chevy II," "Chevelle," and "Caprice." The name selected—"Camaro"—had additional appeal for the gun-shy corporation in that it wasn't commonly used in the English language and thus couldn't piss off Ralph Nader. General Motors marketers found the name in the 1935 edition of *Heath's French to English Dictionary*, which defined the word as: "friend, pal, or comrade," words that even the nervous Mr. Nader wouldn't find offensive.

Like other vehicles in the pony car genre, the Camaro leaned more toward 2+2 seating rather than true four-seating capability. Factor in the smallish trunk, and the result was a great weekend-getaway car, rather than a cross-country hauler.

On June 28, 1966, Pete Estes, by that time Chevrolet Division's general manager, contacted automotive editors from magazines and newspapers in 14 major U.S. markets and officially announced the upcoming Camaro, which he described as a logical follow-up to the Corvette and Corvair Monza. Mr. Estes inducted all participants in the conference call, which in itself was a historic technological undertaking that required extensive expertise from Ma Bell, into a club called SEPAW, or Society for the Elimination of Panthers from the Automotive World. Estes told society members that this was their inaugural and final meeting, then introduced the Camaro name. He made no mention of the Mustang, but he didn't have to make the comparison. By that time, Ford had sold more than 1 million Mustangs, making it the most ubiquitous new car in America.

Pontiac's F-Body

Midway through development of Chevrolet Division's upcoming F car, GM management decided Pontiac should build its own version of the platform. John DeLorean, who had succeeded Pete Estes as manager of Pontiac Division (and who would later replace Estes at Chevrolet Division), had been trying to get a European-style, lightweight, two-seat sports car approved for several years. By March of 1966, DeLorean's badgering had annoyed GM Executive Vice President Ed Cole so much that, as reported in Gary Witzenburg's book *Firebird*, Cole told DeLorean, "You can take the Camaro and make a car out of that. End of discussion."

GM management wanted Pontiac to release its version of the F car in the fall of 1966, at the same time that Chevrolet released the Camaro, but that would not be possible unless Pontiac simply rebadged a version of the Chevy. DeLorean insisted that his division's F car be uniquely Pontiac and not simply a rehashed Chevrolet. He arranged for a six-month delay in the introduction of Pontiac's F car.

In order to deliver consistently accurate shifts, a Hurst unit is the preferred product. Chevrolet fitted each 1967 Camaro SS with a horn button wearing the SS logo. For the 1967 model year, Chevrolet sold 29,270 examples of the Camaro SS350.

Red-stripe D70x14 two-ply bias-ply tires were standard with the 1967 Camaro SS package. Directional stability with these tires on substandard surfaces was a constant source of gallows humor. Also standard were front fender cubic-inch callouts.

Opposite: Every 1967 Super Sport Camaro was fitted with the F41 Suspension Package, which included heavy-duty shock absorbers and springs. A traction bar was fitted to the passenger side of the rear suspension in an effort to tame axle hop.

Because the basic design was finalized for all practical purposes, Pontiac didn't have a lot of options for making its version of the F car unique, even with a six-month extension. Reshaping sheet metal was out of the question, so Pontiac designers were relegated to reshaping the nose and tail sections of the car.

Pontiac used most of its limited development time to improve the Camaro's suspension. The rear suspension received the bulk of Pontiac engineers' attention. Chevrolet had used a pair of single-leaf tapered springs to suspend the Camaro's rear axle. This reduced manufacturing costs dramatically but reduced the ability to tune the rear suspension in equal measure. When trying to put down the power of one of Chevy's potent V-8 engines, the Camaro's original rear suspension hopped and shook like a tweaking meth fiend. Pontiac developed a more expensive multileaf spring that allowed variable spring ratios in its F car, but these weren't ready in time for the car's debut in early 1967. The more advanced multileaf springs would appear on the 1968 models.

Pontiac's chassis engineers made a number of suspension changes to address the ferocious wheel hop the Camaro experienced under acceleration and, to a lesser degree, under braking. By the time the Pontiac F car went on sale, division engineers had installed an adjustable radius rod on all but the base model (Pontiac used a pair of rods on the high-performance models). This rod helped tame the rear end somewhat, but Pontiac had a more effective cure under development. A staggered-shock arrangement, with the passenger-side shock ahead of the rear axle and the driver-side shock behind it, prevented the axle from rotating, largely eliminating the tendency of the axle

The most visible components of the Rally Sport option were the hidden headlights. On an SS model, the Super Sport nomenclature took precedence over the RS package; hence the use of the SS badging instead of RS badging.

to hop under stress. Like the multileaf springs, this design would not be ready in time for the initial car's debut but would appear on the 1968 model. Except for the addition of radius rods, 1967 Pontiac F cars had to make due with the Camaro's economy-car rear suspension design.

Pontiac's developments paid off, not just for the division's Firebird, but also for the Camaro. Much of Pontiac's development work would be adapted to future high-performance Camaros.

Panther on the Prowl

Chevrolet released a fleet of Camaros to the press on September 12, 1966 and examples hit the showrooms on September 29. By that time, the American public was as spastic with anticipation for the new Chevy as was the automotive press. In its November 1966 issue, *Hot Rod* magazine called the Camaro " '67's most anticipated car."

Chevrolet initially offered the car in two configurations—coupe and convertible— and with three trim levels: Sport Coupe, Rally Sport, and Super Sport.

Traditional pony car proportions were maintained on the 1967 Camaro, including the long hood/short deck. Having a large hood helps when installing a large engine. Chevrolet made sure that its new car could handle a big-block engine.

Above: Pitting a Chevrolet V-8 against bias-ply tires rarely worked out in favor of the rolling stock. During the era, stopping a pony car in fewer than 150 feet from 60 miles per hour was considered an accomplishment.

Opposite: Chevrolet used two different nose bumblebee stripes, available in either white or black, on the 1967 Camaro SS. It was available for installation on all Camaros as RPO D91, a $14.75 option.

The base Sport Coupe, priced at $2,466, undercut the price of the least-expensive Mustang, which cost $2,510. Its computer-tuned suspension might not have been up to the standards set by European sport coupes, or even the Corvette, which had yet to earn the international reputation it holds today, but it was much smoother and better-controlled than the rough-riding Mustang, a car with a suspension that was very little changed from its Falcon progenitor. More importantly, the handling of the new Camaro was safer than small cars that had come before it, particularly the Corvair, which meant that the Camaro wouldn't be yet another stick up Ralph Nader's butt.

General Motors had good reason to cater to the portion of the public demanding safer cars. Thanks in large part to the publication of *Unsafe at Any Speed*, these folks had gained the ear of the federal government, which was writing new regulations regarding automotive safety each year. The first wave of these rules took effect for the 1967 model year and led to a host of features found on the new Camaro: dual hydraulic

Tom McCahill of *Mechanix Illustrated* ran a 1967 Camaro SS350 through its paces, reaching 60 miles per hour in eight seconds and covering the quarter-mile in 15.9 seconds. He reported that the top speed was in excess of 118 miles per hour. Dan Gurney, writing for *Popular Mechanics*, reached 60 miles per hour in 7.3 seconds.

braking circuits splitting the front and rear brakes, brake-system warning lights, hazard flashers, front-seat backrest latches, and integrated attachments for optional front-seat shoulder harnesses. Nader may have been a nuisance to General Motors, but in all fairness, most of these safety technologies were extremely beneficial for the driving public. General Motors also introduced mesh-type collapsible steering colums on nearly all its vehicles in 1967, an important safety technology pioneered by GM.

The base engine in the Sport Coupe was a 140-horsepower, 230-cubic-inch version of Chevrolet's long-running inline six. This well-built engine featured seven main bearings, as did the optional 155-horsepower, 250-cubic-inch six. Both were strong enough to handle any performance part that could be bolted on; but by late 1966 no one was hopping up six-cylinder engines, which were about as cool as taking your mom to your prom. While it only cost $26.35 to upgrade to the more powerful six, making the additional 15 horsepower and 20 cubic inches relative bargains, most people who would be swayed by this economy were probably shopping for homely Chevy IIs, or perhaps AMC Ramblers. These folks did not comprise the Camaro's target market.

The checkered flag on the 1967 Camaro SS350 front fender was a corporate wish as the Chevrolet pony car hit the racetrack. In actuality, the Z28 was the recipient of Chevy's efforts to make the Camaro competitive on the track.

It wasn't that the six-cylinder versions had nothing to offer; they were actually quite good cars, and even the base 140-horsepower version cranked out 220 lb-ft of torque. They were far from fast, but at least the six-cylinder models could get out of their own way. In a road test for its July 1968 issue, *Motor Trend* coaxed a Camaro equipped with the 155-horsepower, 250-cubic-inch six backed by a two-speed Powerglide through the quarter-mile in 18.7 seconds, almost as fast as the first V-8-powered Novas of just three years earlier.

The six-cylinder Camaros might not have terrorized the local citizenry with their tire-shredding performance in stoplight drag races, but in some ways they were even better than the V-8 versions. Weighing less than the V-8 cars (2,998 pounds versus 3,210 pounds for the SS350) and with less weight over the front wheels (54.9/45.1 percent versus 57.5/42.5 percent for the SS350), the six-cylinder Camaros proved to be more balanced and better-handling cars. Thanks to reduced weight, the six-cylinder cars stopped better too, at least compared to V-8 cars with standard drum brakes. Plus,

Sales of the 1967 Camaro SS350 far outstripped sales of the big-block SS396, introduced later in the model year. A $210.65 option, the 350-cubic-inch L48 was a durable and healthy powerplant.

A soft tonneau cover over the folded convertible stack maintained the sleek looks on the 1967 Camaro SS350. The smallish trunk became even more diminutive with the soft top, but buyers didn't mind, as 19,856 V-8 convertibles were sold.

the six-cylinder cars were much more miserly with a gallon of gas. *Car Life* magazine averaged 19.2 miles per gallon with a 250-cubic-inch car in its March 1967 road test. But in 1966, good gas mileage, like a six-cylinder engine, was for geeks. In 1960, 47 percent of Chevrolet customers ordered cars equipped with V-8 engines; by 1965, the percentage demanding V-8s had increased to 67.

Camaro Motivation

Nongeek Camaro buyers skipped past the 250-cubic-inch six on the option sheet and checked the box for a V-8. In the Sport Coupe, this meant Chevrolet's 327-cubic-inch

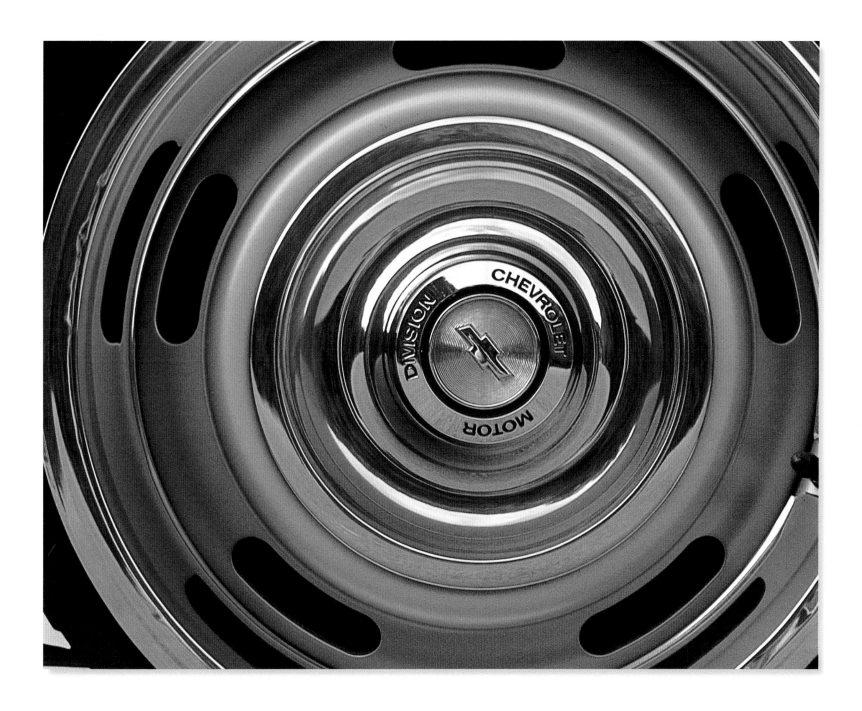

unit. For anyone without embalming fluid flowing through their veins, this proved to be $106 well spent. A buyer willing to spend $2,572 received a 210-horsepower small-block V-8 topped by a two-barrel carburetor. With bore and stroke dimensions of 4.00 inches and 3.25 inches, respectively, this oversquare engine revved willingly and provided 320 lb-ft of torque, enough to lay dark stripes on the pavement all the way from the drive-in to the Standard Oil station down the block—at least as long as it wasn't hooked up to the antiquated two-speed Powerglide slush-box transmission, the only available automatic transmission at the time of the car's launch. The standard transmission on the Sport Coupe was a fully synchronized three-speed manual

Simple, clean, and lightweight, these wheel covers on the 1967 Camaro SS350 were the same as those found on the 1967 Corvette. They were also found on Z28s. Fourteen-inch wheels left a lot of room for rubber.

Being a mass-produced vehicle, the 1967 Camaro SS350 occasionally suffered from less-than-perfect part alignment. This extended to the headlight doors on Rally Sport–equipped cars. When these automobiles are restored, often the parts end up fitting far better than when new.

that came with a column-mounted shifter, which *Car Life* said was "as horrible as ever." When ordered with an optional floor-mounted shifter, the three-speed was an adequate transmission, though far from outstanding. In the spring of 1967 Chevrolet marketed a sporty six-cylindar Camaro called the "Pacer" (perhaps an allusion to the Camaro's pacing of that year's Indianapolis 500), which featured a floor-mounted three-speed manual transmission as standard equipment, along with an SS-like bumble bee stripe.

The Powerglide, a $194.85 option on the V-8-powered cars, was meant for wimps who did not know how to drive a stick, and the three-speed was for nerds who were probably shopping for a Chevy II or a Rambler anyway. Anyone with at least one functioning testicle (75 percent of first-generation Camaro buyers were male) ponied up $184.35 and ordered the optional four-speed tranny. Two versions of the Muncie four-speed transmission were available: the standard wide-ratio unit (coded M20) and a close-ratio gearbox (coded M21). People mistakenly assumed that the close-ratio unit was the high-performance setup, and it was, if you hauled your car to the track and

Even though the SS badging superseded the RS badging on vehicles equipped with both option packages, the black-painted rear light trim from the RS package was retained. Super Sport badging on the fuel filler cap was standard.

Matador Red, paint code RR, was a popular color on the 1968 Camaro SS350. Conventional grilles on the '68 Camaro exhibited a more pronounced V, a styling element that would be revived for the new fifth-generaton Camaro.

only drove on road courses. If you stopped and started, especially if you started quickly enough to light up the rear tires in billowy plumes of smoke and continued to keep your foot in the carburetor until the guy beside you receded in your rearview mirror, you wanted the lower first-gear ratio offered by the wide-ratio gear set.

The four-barrel version of the 327-cubic-inch V-8 topped the engine option sheet for the base Sport Coupe. This optional engine, given the internal code L30, cost

A variation of the bumblebee stripe from 1967 debuted on the 1968 Camaro SS. The stripe ended halfway down the front fender and extended down the vehicle side to a point just in front of the trailing edge of the door.

$92.70 and cranked out 275 horsepower and 355 lb-ft of torque. The L30 version of the Sport Coupe received little attention from the press, which focused on the top SS350 model when Chevrolet launched the Camaro, and legitimate road-test performance numbers are hard to come by, though anyone who has driven one knows they were plenty fast. A properly set up L30 was, for all practical purposes, a bargain-priced Super Sport without the "SS" badges.

The Phantom Super Sport

Chevrolet never made a Super Sport version of the Camaro with an L30 engine, but to this day a core group of Camaro enthusiasts believe that such a beast existed. This situation came about because of an advertising snafu. In 1967, Chevrolet ran Camaro ads showing a car with SS-like stripes and "327" engine badges. To make matters more confusing, the ad copy mistakenly proclaimed the car an SS.

In reality, the car featured a combination of option packages—primarily the L30 engine combined with the M20 transmission—that created a car that was just a few horsepower shy of being an SS350. Beyond the racing stripes, 275-horse engine, and Muncie four-speed transmission signified by the option codes, the L30/M20 combination featured a number of improvements that were standard equipment in the SS350 version of the Camaro. These included the F41 suspension package with stiffer springs and shocks and the right-side radius rods designed to help tame the rear axle, as well as a heavy-duty 12-bolt rear end.

Camaro SS350

At the time of the Camaro's September 1966 launch, the SS350 version of the car topped the performance ladder. This car followed Chevrolet's standard Super Sport formula: add special "SS" badges to the front grille, the rear-mounted gas cap, and as many surfaces in between as practical. In addition, the Camaro SS350 features bodacious striping, introducing what would become a staple for other SS models in Chevrolet's lineup. In the case of the new Camaro, the stripe around the nose of the car was inspired by the paint scheme of older fighter planes, which had the aluminum on their nose pieces painted to cut down on reflected glare. To further differentiate the SS version of the Camaro, Chevy designers mounted a pair of simulated chrome vents on the hood.

By the mid 1960s, Super Sport had also come to signify a certain level of performance in Chevrolet's cars, and the SS350 was no exception. The car would be the showcase for the newest and largest small-block V-8 engine Chevrolet had ever produced up until that time. Chevrolet only offered one version of this engine in the fall of 1966, and it was only available in the Camaro SS350. This high-performance small-block, given the engine code "L48," generated a respectable 295 horsepower and 380 lb-ft of torque when topped by a Rochester four-barrel carburetor. Hydraulic lifters kept maintenance simple, and the engine returned an acceptable 16 to 19 miles per gallon under normal driving conditions. Kick in the secondary jets on the four-barrel carb, and the gas gauge went down almost as fast as the speedometer went up. As *Road & Track* magazine noted: "Gas mileage? Who cares?"

In addition to the standard F41 suspension package, the SS350 featured D70x14 wide-oval red-stripe tires on 6-inch rims. Like the F41 suspension, this wheel-and-tire combination was available as on option on base Sport Coupes.

Car Life magazine coaxed a 15.8-second quarter-mile time out of the SS350, going from 0 to 60 in just 7.8 seconds, when it tested the car for its March 1967 issue.

Car and Driver matched that 7.8-second 0-to-60 time when it tested an SS350 for its November 1967 issue but could only manage to make it through the quarter-mile traps in 16.1 seconds. The testers at *Hot Rod* magazine had a bit more experience in flogging a car through the quarter-mile and attained a 15.05-second elapsed time in a bone-stock car. When they advanced the distributor curve and changed spark plugs, they brought that time down to 14.95 seconds.

Rally Sport

Chevy designers understood the importance of making their new pony car esthetically appealing. Toward that end, they developed a special appearance group that was unique to the Camaro: the Rally Sport package. Chevrolet offered this package independently of any mechanical options and, at the time of the Camaro's September 1966 launch date, it could be ordered on any car, from a base Sport Coupe to an SS350.

There is some evidence that Chevrolet originally intended the components of the RS package to be standard equipement on all Camaros, but the components were so expensive that they would have pushed Camaro prices higher than Mustang prices. Thus the components became part of the optional RS packages.

Given the content of the RS package, its $105.35 list was a considerable bargain. The most distinctive part of the package was the special grille with doors that covered the headlights when not in use. These electrically powered doors blended in with the rest of the grille when closed and opened sideways, toward the center of the grille, where they were hidden behind the grille when opened. Other features of the RS package included parking lights built into the front valence beneath the bumper, backup lights mounted in the rear valence, and "RS" emblems on the grille, fender, steering wheel, and gas filler cap. If an SS350 was ordered with the RS option, the SS emblems took the place of the RS emblems in those locations.

The combination of coupe or convertible, the Rally Sport package, four optional engines, and a Super Sport version (on top of which could be added the Rally Sport appearance package), meant Chevrolet provided buyers with a wide variety of choices from the very first day the car was launched. Overall buyers responded well to the new car, buying 94,417 Camaros in calendar year 1966, good numbers to be sure, but not the sort of numbers that had Ford fearing for the survival of its Mustang, which was on track to sell 472,121 units for the 1967 model year. While the initial Camaro offerings were good, more would be needed. Fortunately, Chevrolet had much more on the way.

Opposite: RPO option C08—the vinyl roof cover—cost $73.75. Staggered rear shocks and multileaf rear springs were standard on the 1968 Camaro SS in an effort to improve traction under heavy throttle.

CHAPTER TWO

GIVING THE CAMARO SOME BERRIES

Looking little like a hand grenade with the pin pulled, the 1969 Camaro ZL-1 was in fact a race car with license plate frame. Only 69 were built, each equipped with a 427-cubic-inch aluminum-block, aluminum-head engine and intake manifold to save critical weight.

The Camaro debuted to a generally positive response, but sales started off a bit slow. Overall, reviewers liked the new car, though most agreed that it was not the quantum leap over the Mustang that many fans had hoped for. In its November 1966 issue, *Hot Rod* judged the Camaro good enough to "quell Ford's Mustang sales" and "give the horse a good run for its money," but Chevrolet needed more than "good enough" to compete with Ford's hot-selling pony car.

The SS version in particular was well received, even though the 350 engine suffered some teething problems. Under hard acceleration, the crankshaft could break on early 350-equipped cars. Don McPherson's development team cured this flaw by strengthening the crankshafts, but the car suffered other problems, too. In an owner's report published in the July 1967 issue of *Popular Mechanics*, the majority (60.37 percent) of Camaro owners reported mechanical problems. "Computer analysis played a key role in designing Chevy's new sportster," the magazine stated, "but

Above: The ZL-1 script on the functional cowl induction hood was owner-installed. Factory ZL-1s came with no exterior markings that might tip off competing vehicles. They were truly wolves in sheeps' clothing.

Left: Bearing the "Winters" snowflake casting emblem, the aluminum heads on a 1969 Camaro ZL-1 contained huge intake (2.30-inch) and exhaust (1.88-inch) valves that used exceptionally high lift (0.579 intake, 0.620 exhaust) to feed the gaping 116.8-cc open combustion chambers.

Soon after the Camaro debuted in 1967, it was the lucky recipient of the race-bred 396-cubic-inch big-block V-8. This engine carried over to the 1968 model year, where it was available with three outputs: 325, 350, and 375 horsepower.

Camaro owners report just enough went awry to prove these electronic marvels aren't foolproof."

The most frequent problem reported was the failure of the headlight doors on models equipped with the RS appearance package (32.9 percent). The second most common complaint involved transmission problems (16.5 percent). The article doesn't specify which transmission caused the most problems, but the smart money is on the outdated Powerglide.

The most frequent complaints about the car revolved around the Chevy II-sourced rear suspension, which was described as "flimsy" and "skittish." An Iowa owner reported: "Traction from a dead stop is nonexistent." An owner from Missouri reported that the "rear end hops and winds up like a yo-yo under normal acceleration."

One positive note in the *Popular Mechanics* report was that the car was a hit with its intended audience. Most buyers (55.7 percent) were 29 years old or younger, putting them squarely in the baby-boom generation. Still, the Camaro was not the home run General Motors had hoped for. One obvious reason was that, with the Mustang, Chevy had taken a shot at a moving target. In most respects, the Camaro represented an improvement over the 1964 1/2 Mustang. If the Camaro had debuted at the same time as Ford's Mustang 2 1/2 years earlier, it may have been the defining automobile of the baby-boom generation. But the Camaro was not competing against that earlier Mustang; it was competing against a redesigned 1967 Mustang. The new Mustang had

more contemporary styling, more features, and most importantly, a new engine: the big-block 390.

While Ford's advanced thin-wall casting technique had resulted in a lightweight V-8 engine that fit within the tight confines of the Falcon engine bay, its big-block engines were still large and heavy and needed more elbow room than the original Mustang could provide. Fitting one of the beasts in a 1964 1/2 to 1966 Mustang was out of the question, so for the 1967 model year, Ford designers widened the Mustang by over 2.5 inches, opening up just enough space in the engine bay to drop a big-block V-8. That is exactly what they did. For an additional $232, a Mustang buyer could order a 320-horsepower, 390-cubic-inch big-block and transform his pony car into a genuine muscle car. While the new mill only generated 25 more horsepower than the Camaro's

In an effort to control axle hop under heavy acceleration, staggered rear shock absorbers were introduced on the 1968 model year Camaro. The driver-side shock was mounted ahead of the solid rear axle, while the passenger-side shock was installed aft of the axle housing.

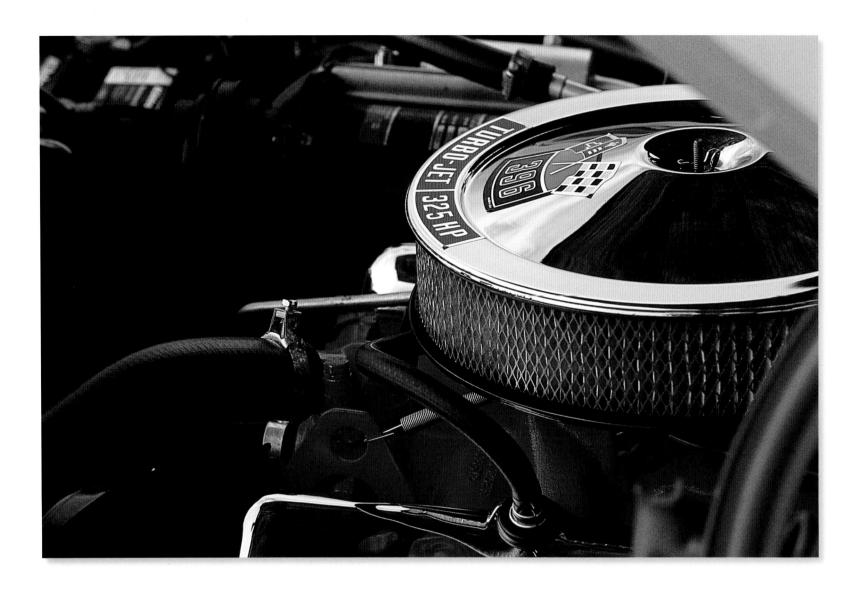

Big-block engines in the 1968 Camaro SS required a lot of fresh air, and the large, open-element air cleaner fit the bill. Chevrolet built 10,773 1968 Camaro SS models equipped with the 396-/325-horsepower L35 option.

small-block 350, it pumped out a massive 427 lb-ft of torque, the twisting force that made exiting a high-school parking lot a much more antisocial event. Clearly, excessive power and torque sold cars. Ford sold nearly two Mustangs for every Camaro sold by Chevrolet in 1967—417,121 units versus 220,906 units, respectively. Making the Mustang bigger and badder had been a good move.

A Truly Super Super Sport

The press responded to the Camaro in a generally positive fashion, but from the September 1966 introduction of the car, reporters began asking about the availability of a big-block Camaro. Chevrolet promised to have such a car on the market by the end of the calendar year. GM management knew that if the Camaro was to compete against the Mustang, it too would have to feature an excessively large optional engine. For this reason, Chevrolet designers had given the Camaro's engine compartment enough room to accept any of the division's V-8 engines, including the mack-daddy 427-cubic-inch

Simulated air intakes on the top of the hood were part of the 1968 Camaro SS option, regardless of engine displacement. The Camaro adhered to the long hood/short deck pony car formula.

big-block available in the Corvette and Impala SS427, so installing a larger engine presented no technological challenges. Chevrolet engineers promised to give the Camaro an engine capable of beating any stock 390-powered Mustang.

Chevrolet kept its word and, in December 1966, the Camaro SS received the division's L35 engine—a 396-cubic-inch, 325-horsepower street-going version of Chevrolet's awe-inspiring 427-cubic-inch Mark II racing motor—as a $263.30 option. If an owner was willing to deal with the hassle of mechanical lifters instead of hydraulic lifters and had the financial means to shell out an additional $237, he could get the 375-horsepower L78 version of the engine. This stout engine, with its four-bolt main bearings, revved like few other big-block engines of the period and has to rank as one of the all-time great street engines ever to grace the engine bay of an American performance car. Like the 390-cubic-inch rendition of the Mustang, the 396-cubic-inch version of the Camaro SS pushed Chevy's pony car squarely into the muscle car ranks.

Part of the 1968 Camaro Super Sport package was the nose-mounted bumblebee stripe. In the latter portion of the model year, the stripe extended aft, ending at the rear edge of the door.

While the handsome interior was billed as a four-seater, like most pony cars, it was actually a 2+2. The rear seats were suitable for children, groceries, and people you didn't like.

Since there was no possible way that Chevrolet's archaic Powerglide transmission could withstand the L35's 410 lb-ft of torque, much less the 415 lb-ft of churning force cranked out by the L78, the division offered the excellent three-speed Turbo Hydramatic transmission as a $226.45 option.

The base L35 wasn't that much faster than the SS350, at least in stock form, but if a buyer knew how to work Chevrolet's option list and parts counter, the SS396 became a serious drag racer. If a buyer ordered option G80—a Posi-Traction rear axle that listed for $42.15—and equipped it with one of the optional nonstandard gear sets, particularly option code H05, a 3.73:1 ratio gear set that cost a whopping $2.15, the owner ended up with a very quick automobile. For a serious hot rodder, this represented a much more sensible expenditure than the Comfortilt steering column. The really serious hot rodder could get gear sets from a Chevrolet parts man with ratios up to a bulldozer-like 4.88:1. *Motor Trend* described this setup as "designed expressly for the man who wants to get away in a hurry."

The rear spoiler (option code D80) was standard on the Z28, but for $32.65 it could fitted to any Camaro. A black valence panel between the rear lights was standard on Super Sport Camaros packing the big-block engine.

Chevrolet used the 1967 running of the Indianapolis 500-mile race to showcase the new Camaro. This convertible was the actual pace car for the race, with a blueprinted and run-in 396-cubic-inch V-8 under the hood.

Indianapolis 500 Pace Car

Late in the winter of 1967, Chevrolet announced that a Camaro would be used as the pace car for the running of that year's Indianapolis 500. The Camaros (Chevrolet built three extra examples so there would be two backup cars on race day)—Ermine White SS396 convertibles with RS trim packages—featured blue interiors and were powered by L35 engines backed by Turbo Hydra-Matic transmissions. This would be just the third Chevrolet to pace the historic 500-mile race in its 51-year history. In 1948, a Chevrolet Fleetmaster convertible had paced the race, and in 1955, a Bel Air performed the task. In addition, Chevrolet provided at least 100 look-alike Camaros as courtesy cars to chauffeur track officials, drivers, celebrities, and other prominent people around during the traditional Memorial Day event.

The interior of the 1967 Camaro SS Indianapolis 500 pace car was essentially stock, but note the grab handle where the passenger sun visor would normally be.

As befitted the Indianapolis 500 pace car, this 1967 Camaro SS/RS was loaded with options, such as the Rally Sport package.

Chevrolet milked all the publicity it could from the event, running two-page, full-color ads in the racing programs, strategically placing six Camaro billboards along the highways leading to the track, and taking out a full-page ad in the *Indianapolis Star-News* on race day. Mario Andretti, 1966 USAC National Champion, drove the pace car through a huge poster of a checkered flag, with Chevrolet Division General Manager Pete Estes as his passenger. A marching band performed, and Estes told those gathered how honored Chevrolet was to have the Camaro selected as the pace car. Then a balloonist descended onto the track, and Estes joined officials as they drove the pace car around the track for an official inspection. Cecil B. DeMille would have been impressed.

Chevrolet couldn't have found a better showcase for the new Camaro SS/RS than having it act as the pace car for the 1967 Indianapolis 500-mile race. Dual yellow flags got the attention of race car drivers on the 2 ½-mile oval, while the pace car driver pedaled hard to stay in front.

Given all the hype, Chevrolet chose not to capitalize on the occasion by producing pace car replicas for the public. The only replicas were the 100 or so cars produced to use during the race weekend, which were sold as used cars after the event, along with perhaps another 44 cars that didn't appear at the Indianapolis race, according to internal GM estimates. Perhaps GM management was stung by the criticism that by pacing the race, Chevrolet Division was violating the AMA's 1957 ban on factory involvement in automobile racing. Whatever the reason, Chevrolet would not fail to market replicas to the general public twice.

Option Package Z28

In 1966, the SCCA began running a road-racing series that would prove the ideal arena in which the new pony cars could compete. This series featured sedans with four permanent seats competing in two classes: an amateur class and a professional class. The amateur class comprised a series of regional races, culminating with the top three finishers from six separate regions competing in the American Road Race of Champions

(ARRC). The professional races consisted of longer events, called the Trans-American Sedan Championship, or Trans-Am races.

In addition to awarding a championship to the winning driver at the end of a season, it awarded a championship to the winning manufacturer. This made competing in the series an attractive marketing proposition for U.S. automakers trying to sell pony cars to baby boomers and, in 1966, every manufacturer was either selling or developing such a pony car. The SCCA enforced strict rules in the Trans-Am series—rules intended to keep the cars on the tracks as close as possible to the cars manufactured for street use. This made the series extremely popular with fans across the United States right from the initial series of seven races, and the popularity of the series increased throughout the 1960s.

The predictable result was that every new pony car introduced from 1966 on would include a model or option package designed to homologate the car for Trans-Am racing. Before Chevy's pony car entrant even hit the market, the Bowtie Division had begun developing a Trans-Am homologation package for its Camaro.

Low key and rare: the 1967 Camaro Z28. Chevrolet filled the 302-cubic-inch engine with stout parts in an effort to compete in the SCCA Trans Am series. The first one was built on December 29, 1966, at Chevrolet's Norwood, Ohio, plant.

Chevrolet rated the 1967 Z28 engine at 290 horsepower. Yes, it delivered 290 horsepower, at the rated 5,500 rpm, on its way to producing approximately 350 horsepower for drivers willing to ignore the red hash marks on the tachometer. The race-honed mill would spin to 7,500 revs without a whimper.

At Chevrolet, Vince Piggins managed a department called "product promotion." This was really code for "racing department," a deception necessitated by the fact that General Motors still abided by the AMA racing ban.

By 1966 General Motors corporate management began to look the other way a bit regarding its racing ban. Pete Estes and his Chevrolet Division felt it wise to keep their racing activities as clandestine as possible, but those activities still had to take place. Given the fierce competition the upcoming Camaro would be facing from the Ford Mustang, the Chevy needed all the promotion it could get, so in August 1966, Piggins convinced Estes to develop a racing version of the Camaro for the new Trans-Am series.

Piggins faced a major engineering challenge in finding a suitable engine for the Camaro. The smallest V-8 available in the car—the 327-cubic-inch version—was too large to comply with SCCA's displacement limit of 5 liters, or roughly 305 cubic inches. Piggins' answer was to put a forged version of the cast crankshaft from the 283-cubic-inch small-block V-8 into a modified 327-cubic-inch block, leading to a 302-cubic-inch engine with a bore of 4 inches and a stroke of 3 inches. This oversquare design meant the engine would have a lower piston speed at a given rpm, allowing the engine to have a higher redline.

For all practical purposes, the 302-inch engine in what was officially called "Camaro Sport Coupe with Regular Production Option (RPO) Z28" was a racing engine for the street. (Pete Estes and his team at Chevrolet liked the sound of the RPO name so much that they never gave the car another name.) With 11.0:1-compression forged pistons; a steep, solid-lifter camshaft; an aluminum high-rise intake manifold

Buyers of the 1967 Z28 could get any transmission they wanted as long as it was a four-speed manual with a Hurst shifter. Chevrolet "recommended" Posi-Traction. Makes checking the options list easy.

When the Z28 debuted in 1967, exterior badging was nonexistent. Chevrolet marketing felt that a pair of stripes imparted a sporty look to the hot pony car. Savvy buyers soon found out that the Z28 didn't need stripes to be sporty.

Roger Penske has always run a first-class racing operation, and 1968, when he had Mark Donahue behind the wheel of this race car, was no exception. Donohue clinched the series championship after just 9 races in the 13-race schedule. Here he is seen at the top of the famous Corkscrew turn at the Monterey Historic Races.

designed especially for the 302; and an 800-cfm Holley dual-feed carburetor, the engine specs were more appropriate for a track-bound car than a street-going car. Chevrolet rated torque at 290 lb-ft and claimed a horsepower rating of 290 at 4,000 rpm. That number may have been accurate at 4,000 rpm, but the engine achieved peak power of an estimated 350 horsepower at a race-car-like 7,500 rpm. To gain an instant 60 horsepower, all a driver had to do was run the tach needle into the stratosphere.

To rev that high, the little engine needed to breathe. In addition to the Holley double-pumper perched atop the custom-built high-rise manifold, the engine featured heads with 2.02-inch intake valves and 1.60-inch exhaust valves. These sent spent gases through fat 2.25-inch exhaust dual pipes back to a pair of low-restriction mufflers. A heavy-duty radiator with a five-blade clutch fan kept this high-revving overachiever of an engine cool.

A good suspension meant as much to the Camaro's Trans-Am racing success as a fast engine. Piggins' team started with the best suspension available for the Camaro—the F41—and improved it. The racing version received stiffer rear springs, quicker steering gears, a thicker front anti-roll bar, and a radius rod similar to the one Pontiac was developing for its upcoming Firebird. A stronger rear axle allowed the use of the Corvette's rear disc brakes.

This engine and suspension package had to appear on a street car designed to homologate the Camaro for the Trans-Am series. Cars intended for actual track use received further modifications, like heavy-duty spindles, axles, and shafts, along with special bushings and a 37-gallon fuel cell—a requirement if the car was to be competitive in the long-distance Trans-Am events.

Most options were aimed at on-track performance rather than on-road comfort. Comfort and luxury options such as air conditioning and a convertible body were not even available. Instead, the options list consisted of expensive, hard-core speed equipment, such as a $437.10 air plenum air cleaner assembly and $779.40 exhaust headers. A shrewd buyer ordered these as part of RPO Z28, which, at $858.40 ($421 more than ordering RPO Z28 without these options), amounted to a $795 discount.

Two of the additions stretched the concept of "option," since they were mandatory options: the $121.15 power disc brakes and the $184.35 four-speed transmission, on top of the $358.10 price for the RPO Z28 package

Chevrolet displayed the prototype Camaro Sport Coupe with RPO Z28 at Riverside, California, on November 26, 1966, and built the first production model, a Tuxedo Black car with gold trim, in early December of that year. What Chevrolet advertising called "big, bold stereo stripes" across the hood and trunk lid provided the only outward distinguishing characteristic of RPO Z28. According to the same ad, the stripes served "no mechanical function," but had "great psychological value." That was the Alpha and Omega of the car's list of fluff; every other part of the car had mechanical function up the wazoo.

Drivers who knew how to wring out a peaky, high-revving engine liked the new car. *Car and Driver* magazine called the engine's horsepower rating of 290 "ridiculously conservative," comparing the acceleration of the Z28 to a 426 Hemi.

Sales started out slow. Chevrolet sold just 602 Camaro Sport Coupes with RPO Z28 that first year, which didn't surprise anyone at Chevrolet since the car hadn't been intended as a mass-market transportation device. It had been designed to win races, and Chevrolet needed only sell enough street versions to homologate the car for the Trans-Am series. And it did win races.

Trans-American Sedan Championship

Chevrolet shipped the first production RPO Z28 car built to Aero Chevrolet in Alexandria, Virginia, where Roger Penske took delivery of the car on January 10, 1967. Penske had been named "SCCA Driver of the Year" by *Sports Illustrated* magazine in 1960. He retired from racing in 1965 to focus on building and fielding cars for his own Penske Racing race team. Chevrolet officially still didn't participate in racing and Penske Racing operated as a privateer racing effort. But thanks to the back-door support of people within Chevrolet like Vince Piggins, for all practical purposes, Penske Racing would operate much like a satellite factory racing team in the Trans-Am series.

The first thing Penske did was ship the car to engine-development specialist Henry "Smokey" Yunick for tuning and race preparation. Yunick, a World War II vet who had flown 50-plus missions over Europe as a B-17 pilot, owned a shop in Daytona Beach, Florida, called "Smokey's Best Damn Garage in Town." His Best Damn Garage became a gearhead Mecca, a place where hot rodders from around the country (and around the world) visited whenever they were in town for a race. A successful racer and one of the best builders/tuners in NASCAR history, Yunick was the guy to see if you wanted a car that would win races. Yunick lit into the Camaro, and by the time he was finished, there wasn't much of it that the folks at the Chevrolet plant in Norwood, Ohio, would recognize as their handiwork.

At Daytona, Penske's driver, Mark Donahue, led the first three laps of the first Trans-Am race of the season but retired with engine problems. Donahue later retired from the 24-hour endurance race with transmission problems.

After the race, Penske shipped the car back to Piggins, where his Special Performance group went over the car and developed improved engine, suspension, and brake components to help the car live up to the potential it had shown at Daytona, where Donahue hit 162 miles per hour on the back straight.

By mid-April, Piggins' team still hadn't solved the car's major problems, and the Penske/Donahue effort suffered. The main problem was the same one noted by many of the customers responding to the *Popular Science* owner survey: rear-axle wind up and hop under acceleration and braking.

Piggins' engineers put the Camaro on a radical weight-loss program. They ordered four lightweight Camaro bodies with thinner-gauge metal, which shed 95 pounds. The race teams then acid-dipped the bodies, removing an additional 200 pounds, bringing the Camaro down to the weight of the rival Mustang. This was completely illegal according to SCCA rules, but everyone was doing it. This is why a lot of the cars competing used vinyl roof covers—they overdipped the car bodies in acid and the roof panels got so thin and wavy that the rule violation would be obvious.

Brake lockup had been a problem throughout the season. In an attempt to correct it, Piggins' crew had installed a brake bias valve from the Corvette, but this hadn't helped. It wasn't until the valves had been used in several races that they discovered why they weren't working—they'd been installed backward, sending most of the braking force to the rear brakes instead of the front, which was the exact opposite of the hoped-for results.

By midseason, Chevrolet trailed both Ford and Mercury in manufacturer's points, but the teams finally had the Camaro's suspension sorted out. Donahue finally won a six-hour endurance event at Marlboro, Maryland, and went on to win two more of the remaining five events. It wasn't enough to wrestle the manufacturer's title from Ford, but it boded well for the following season.

Piggins continued to develop the chassis over the winter, and Yunick worked to wring more performance from the 302 engine. Yunick also campaigned his own car, a radical racer of questionable legality. (It had been banned from competing at California's Riverside Raceway in the fall of 1967 for rules violations.) Donahue retired from 1968's opening race at Daytona on February 4 with a cracked cylinder head, but prior to that, the Penske car had dominated the competition. At the 12-hour endurance race in Sebring, Florida, the following month, Penske's cars finished first and second.

Famed race engine builder Traco assembled the potent 302-cubic-inch V-8 that powered the Roger Penske 1969 Trans Am Camaro. Twin Holley four-barrel carburetors helped to generate 440 horsepower.

Donahue continued to dominate the competition for the rest of the season, winning 10 of the 13 races that made up the series, and Penske Racing helped Chevrolet secure the manufacturer's championship title. Mustangs only won two of the three races not won by Donahue, which must have been especially pleasing for Piggins and everyone else at Chevrolet. Camaro sales had picked up in 1968—the division sold a total of 235,147 units for the model year, up from the 220,906 Camaros Chevrolet sold in the 1967 model year—but Ford still outsold Chevrolet in the pony car market, selling 317,404 Mustangs for the model year. If the Mustang was still winning the battle on the showroom floor, at least Chevrolet was kicking Ford's ass on the racetrack.

Cross-Ram

In part, the Camaro's stunning racetrack performance came about as the result of a new intake system that featured two four-barrel Holley carburetors atop a "Cross-Ram" intake manifold. Within weeks of its on-track debut, Chevrolet made this system available through its parts distribution system. The system was complete and included the Holley carburetors and attendant linkage, air cleaner with ducting to the cowl plenum chamber, and, of course, the radical Cross-Ram manifold itself. The kit even included a new oil filler tube, as well as all gaskets, clamps, hoses, fuel lines, springs, brackets, spacers, bolts, and screws, and even the eight nuts needed to bolt on the two carbs. The Cross-Ram intake wouldn't fit under the stock hood, so a buyer would have to install a fiberglass hood, an item that wasn't included in the kit. When Chevrolet warned the kit was for competition use only, it wasn't kidding, because the kit didn't include any provisions for heat tubes or chokes, and it wasn't designed to work very well under 4,000 rpm. Today, an original Cross-Ram kit can net upward of $25,000 on eBay.

Research to improve the Camaro's chances on the racetrack took many turns. Famous race engine builder Smokey Yunick was approached in 1968 and tasked with extracting more power from the 302-cubic-inch engine for the 1969 season.

Smokey Yunick's Hemi

In the fourth week of April 1968, Chevrolet assembled Z/28 VIN 124378N122393, a number you won't find registered with any motor vehicle department; the car has been used for racing since original owner Tom Prather ordered the car, and it has never been licensed for street use. While unusual, this is not what makes this Camaro unique. The service department at the Kansas City dealership where Prather took delivery of the car installed rear disc brakes—again, not unusual—and an electronic fuel pump and special wiring harness. This was a bit more unusual but not unheard of in a car intended for serious competition.

The truly unique component in the car resides under the hood: a specially constructed 302-cubic-inch V-8 engine with aluminum hemi heads. Chevrolet's engineers built three engines to evaluate experimental heads they were considering selling to customers racing in the SCCA Trans-Am series, and this engine was one of the three. As with most good things coming from Chevrolet at the time, these heads were developed by Vince Piggins' Special Performance engineering group.

The heads featured modified hemispherical combustion chambers; like Mopar's 426-cubic-inch Hemi engine, these heads used a semihemispherical design rather than

The Cross-Ram intake manifold that Smokey Yunick used on the hemi-head engines he developed for the Camaro differed from the Cross-Ram system that Chevrolet parts departments sold for Trans Am racing. Yunick built three of these 302-cubic-inch hemis before Chevrolet pulled the plug on the project.

a true hemispherical design. Piggins and his crew of hot-rodding miscreants began working on these heads in June 1968 to combat Ford's new Cleveland engines, which featured better-breathing cylinder heads and had proven formidable competitors in the Trans-Am series.

The design increased top-end horsepower, but with a corresponding loss in torque, lead to a peaky power band that compromised overall on-track performance. By the time the 1969 Trans-Am racing season began, Piggins had abandoned the project, and the heads were never assigned production numbers.

But the basic design showed promise if engineers could make them breathe properly. The heads were designed to work with an aluminum Cross-Ram intake (this was a completely different intake from the Cross-Ram units Chevrolet sold through its parts departments) topped by a pair of Holley carburetors that simply crammed too big a fuel charge into too small a combustion chamber. This packing of the fuel charge took a toll on horsepower and had an even more detrimental effect on torque.

In an attempt to solve this packing problem—and because Piggins' crew had been reassigned to develop street engines that worked with the coming government-mandated unleaded gasoline and smog controls—Chevrolet brought in Smokey Yunick to take over development of the hemi heads. Yunick knew how to tune a pushrod V-8 engine perhaps better than anyone on the planet at that time, and he knew that small-displacement V-8s were not compatible with a hemispherical combustion-chamber shape. Still, he worked to develop the heads and make them function with the small-block Chevy.

Before Yunick could finish his development, Chevrolet pulled the plug and cut off development money for the project. Developing pollution control equipment and engines that could run on unleaded gas was draining too much money from the division, and funds to pay people like Yunick were drying up.

In order to settle up with Yunick, Chevrolet shipped him the three experimental engines in lieu of the money owed him. The last thing Yunick needed was a bunch of engines with a combustion chamber design he considered obsolete. He did some development work on his own, intending to build a larger 350-cubic-inch version that could make better use of the design, but got sidetracked.

Eventually, one of these three engines met its current host in Smokey's garage. Tom Prather raced Z/28 number 124378N122393 in the SCCA Amateur Series in the A-Sedan class until 1977. Both car and driver performed well over the years, holding their own against even the professional teams. In 1977, the car ended up in Smokey's garage, where it came to house one of Yunick's experimental hemi engines. The end result was a pedigreed race car with one of the most exotic and rare experimental racing small-blocks in Chevrolet's history, built by a man with one of the finest pedigrees in American racing history. Talk about one of one.

Quarter-Mile Camaro

While Penske Racing and others earned the Camaro a reputation as a road-racing champion, others championed Chevy's pony car in a more traditionally American form of motorsports: drag racing.

One Camaro driver—Dave Strickler—proved particularly successful in 1968. By 1968, Strickler and his builder/tuner, Bill "Grumpy" Jenkins, had achieved almost legendary status in National Hot Rod Association (NHRA) drag racing. Jenkins-prepared small-block Chevrolet-powered cars regularly dominated American drag strips, beating competitors using such fearsome engines as Chrysler's 426 Hemi.

In 1968, Strickler campaigned *The Old Reliable*, a Jenkins-built Z/28. With Jenkins' tuning, the car consistently turned in quarter-mile times of 11.70 seconds, a considerable feat considering Super Stock rules required the use of the stock carburetor and intake manifold. Strickler made good use of the car's performance potential. Not only did he dominate the Z/28's NHRA Super Stock class; he regularly beat cars from different classes, such as SS396 Camaros. After a successful season, Strickler went on to win one of the NHRA's most prestigious titles: the 1968 Super Stock World Championship, which he secured at Tulsa, Oklahoma, that October.

Running Changes

In mid-model-year 1968, Chevrolet quit referring to the "Camaro Sport Coupe with RPO Z-28" and made the Z/28 an official Camaro model. At that point, the slash between the Z and the 28 appeared on the car for the first time in the form of front fender emblems. Most 1968 changes for the Z/28 consisted of across-the-board changes for the entire Camaro line, notably the exclusion of side vent windows. Like all Camaros, the Z/28 received the staggered shocks developed for the Pontiac Firebird, as well as the multileaf rear springs that graced the L30/M20 version of the Sport Coupe and all Camaro Super Sports beginning that year. The price of the Z/28 package rose to $400.25. Add on the mandatory options—the $184.35 four-speed transmission (a heavy-duty M22 close-ratio four-speed was available for $310.70) and $142.25 J50/J52 power disc brakes—and a Z/28 started at $3,396.84 and went up from there.

Serious drivers, especially those who spent any time on a racetrack that had both left and right turns, considered the Z/28 *the* Camaro to have. Magazine writers practically coiled themselves over the car. A test of the Z/28 in the June 1968 issue of *Road & Track* stated: "If this isn't a bona fide racing car—in street clothing for this test—then we've never seen one . . . The engine makes no bones about its character . . . The headers give it a nice, tingly sound . . . Chevrolet obviously achieved what they set out to do—namely, building a race-winning Trans-Am sedan."

A month later, *Car Life* tested a Z/28. The magazine reported: "This car needs to be driven, in every sense of the word. To the man capable of extracting them, the Z/28 has a storeroom of treasures. For enjoyment-per-dollar, the Z/28 must be one of the bargains of the decade." Apparently, many buyers agreed with that statement, and they made the Z/28 a resounding sales success in its second year. The combination of racing success, promotion, good word-of-mouth, and perhaps the inclusion of the sexy slash helped sales increase more than tenfold in one year to 7,199 units.

1968 Upgrades

The Z/28 hogged most of the limelight in 1968, but other models received significant upgrades, too. The six-cylinder models offered a unique new transmission, dubbed the "Torque-Drive" by Chevrolet's engineers. This semiautomatic transmission, coded RPO MB1, was basically the two-speed Powerglide with all the mechanical parts needed to shift automatically removed. The driver was required to shift from first to second manually using the column-mounted shifter, the only shifter available with the Torque-Drive. The only real advantage this unit offered was its price: $68.65 versus the $184.35 Powerglide. Chevrolet sold 3,099 Torque-Drive-equipped Camaros in 1968 and dropped the option after the 1969 model year. Most people wanted either a manual transmission or an automatic transmission and weren't interested in a hermaphroditic combination of the two systems.

For buyers wanting something between the base L35 396 and the potent L78, with its maintenance-intensive solid lifters, Chevrolet offered the 350-horsepower L34. This engine featured the same hot-rod parts that made the L78 such a powerhouse—big four-barrel carburetor, strengthened block, and steep cam—but that cam acted on more user-friendly hydraulic lifters.

Another unique option that became available in 1968 was cloth seat inserts with a black-and-white or parchment-and-white checked pattern. In 1969, this striking interior, officially called "houndstooth," would also be available in yellow-and-black and orange-and-black combinations.

Bunkie Bails

In late 1967, GM's directors passed over Semon E. "Bunkie" Knudsen, a genuine car enthusiast who had encouraged the creation of the Camaro, for the position of corporation president. Ford Motor Company quickly snapped up Knudsen and made him the president of Ford Division. Now Knudsen, who was fully aware of Chevrolet's product lineup for the next several years, planned to exact revenge on his former employer.

Knudsen knew that the most expedient way to trump GM was to exploit the company's squeamishness regarding muscle cars. He was particularly interested in an existing project that mounted the company's 428 Cobra Jet engine in the Mustang pony car. Though conservatively rated at 335 horsepower (real output was closer to 400 horsepower), the new 428 Cobra Jet–powered Mustang had the beans to brutalize Camaros. *Hot Rod* magazine tested a Mustang with the 428CJ powerplant and achieved 0 to 60 miles per hour in 5.9 seconds and standing-start quarter-mile runs at 106.6 miles per hour in 13.56 seconds.

The new 428CJ-powered Mustang was a real blow to Camaro fans, but Knudsen was cooking up even more revenge against GM. In 1969, Ford offered a pair of Mustangs carrying Knudsen's nickname: "Boss." The first car, the Boss 302, was a purposeful racer designed to win Trans-Am championships. The second, the Boss 429, was a balls-to-the-wall muscle car designed to homologate Ford's new NASCAR engine. NASCAR required minimum production numbers of any engine to qualify for racing, so Ford offered the 429, rated conservatively at 375 horsepower, in the Boss 429 version of the Mustang, beginning in 1969.

As the decade wound down, Ford offered two optional engines displacing well over 400 cubic inches in its Mustang pony car and the largest regular production engine that Chevrolet offered was still only 396 cubic inches. The Boss 302 was a match for any Z/28, on the road or on the track, and the Boss 429 out-powered any Camaro that Chevrolet officially offered for sale to the public.

COPO

Buyers clamored for a Camaro to compete with the potent big-block Mustangs coming from Ford, but GM management refused to relent on its rules dictating that the Camaro could not have an engine larger than 400 cubic inches. General Motors' reluctance frustrated many Camaro fans, but where most saw obstacles, others saw opportunities. Chevrolet possessed the engines needed to compete—427-inchers ranging from the pedestrian L36, which generated 390 horsepower and 460 lb-ft of torque, to the insane ZL-1, the ultimate expression of the 427-cubic-inch big-block engine and the most exotic pushrod V-8 engine ever produced by an American auto manufacturer.

Unlike Ford's trio of Mustang body designs, the Chevrolet Camaro was offered in two body styles: coupe and convertible. Both offered brawny good looks that have kept the Camaro one of the most desired vehicles ever built. All SS Camaros incorporated faux carburetor inlets on the hood, while COPO Camaros used a ducted hood.

The public embraced the 1969 Camaro in larger numbers than previous years, as 243,085 units were sold for this model year. It was the first year that variable-ratio power steering was available on the sporty Camaro.

The standard engine in the 1969 Camaro SS was the 300-horsepower, 350-cubic-inch V-8. At the other end of the factory-offered RPO powerplants was the 375-horsepower, 396-cubic-inch engine.

Buyers willing to shell out nearly $1,000 over the purchase price of a Camaro could receive a version of the solid-lifter 396 engine with aluminum L89 heads. These L89 engines generated the same 375 horsepower and 415 lb-ft of torque as the L78 engines, but the aluminum shaved off some pounds, an important consideration for drag racers.

A big-block V-8 needs a big carburetor. The 375-horsepower L89 396-cubic-inch engine boasted aluminum heads and cost a lofty $710.95. Until the engine warmed up, it tended to pop and sputter, sounding like it had a leaking exhaust system.

The ZL-1 was one of the most technologically advanced engines produced in the 1960s. Except for the forged-steel crankshaft, connecting rods, and camshaft, almost every part of the engine was made of aluminum, including the 12.25:1-compression pistons and cylinder heads. The entire engine weighed about the same as one of Chevrolet's small-block V-8s.

It was easily the most exclusive engine ever offered by an American auto manufacturer. The only car to receive the ZL-1 engine as a regular production option was the 1969 Corvette, and only two buyers checked the ZL-1 option box when ordering cars that year. This was not a surprising number, given that the $4,718.35 engine roughly doubled the price of the already-expensive Corvette. In all, Chevrolet built a total of 154 ZL-1 engines, most of which ended up in purpose-built racing cars.

A hard-core contingent of Camaro fans clamored for cars with engines to compete against Ford's 428CJ and Boss 429 Mustangs. As early as 1968, Chevrolet made some of its more exotic 396-inch engines available as regular production options on the Camaro, allowing L89 aluminum heads to be installed on the L78 version of the Camaro engine, for example. These made great race engines but weren't great on the street. The aluminum heads and cast-iron blocks heated up at different rates. Since aluminum expands much more than cast iron when warm, tolerances weren't

fully up to spec until the engines were at operating temperature, making these cars temperamental when first started. Just 272 buyers spent the $868.95 needed to get L89 heads in 1968. If the average buyer wanted a larger engine, he either had to do without or install the engine himself. But for the more resourceful Camaro fans, there were alternatives.

Chevrolet had a clandestine system for combining its engines with just about any of its cars, including the Camaro: the Central Office Production Order (COPO) program. This program provided equipment not deemed useful for cars sold to the general public such as special paint schemes for fleet vehicles and heavy-duty suspension parts and durable interior fabrics for taxicabs, but it also included high-performance parts for police use. COPO provided an ideal means through which Chevrolet's renegade engineers could circumvent the corporate ban on racing and supply speed equipment to racers.

Above: Squaring the shape of the wheel openings for the 1969 model year gave the Camaro a more aggressive look. The Super Sport option was very popular in 1969, with 34,932 units sold.

Next page: The 1969 Camaro SS L89 was the perfect blend of visual and performance punch. A surprising number of buyers—100,602—spent the $84.30 for a vinyl roof.

While the 1969 Camaro SS could corner with the best of its era, virtually all performance vehicles at that time had good-looking seats that offered no lateral support. Seatbelts and a firm grip on the steering wheel were needed to stay in place.

Vince Piggins made good use of COPO. Essentially, once Piggins and his cadre of engineers created some wicked-fast prototype, Piggins called certain dealers in major metropolitan areas. He knew the owners already had high-performance customers with deep pockets. Piggins told dealers about the new car or a new engine and asked them how many they would take.

Piggins and other rebels within Chevrolet used COPO to build the image of Chevy cars like the Camaro in an attempt to take a bite out of Mustang sales.

As in prior years, Chevrolet painted the rear panel between the taillights black on the SS 396. Narrow Polyglas tires were state-of-the-art in 1969, offering great looks with middling traction.

Take a Camaro, yank the engine, and replace it with an L72 427-cubic-inch V-8 from a Corvette. In a nutshell, you have the business case for Chevrolet dealer Don Yenko. Only 54 speed-crazed customers took Yenko Camaros home in 1967.

Dealer Specials and Tuner Cars

Some of the biggest Chevy boosters were also Chevrolet dealers, and some of the more resourceful of these decided to do something about the sorry fact that Ford dealers had big-inch Mustangs while Chevy dealers did not offer similar Camaros. These Chevy dealers didn't have the direct support of the factory, as Carroll Shelby had when building his 428-cubic-inch GT500 Mustangs, but they had the next best thing: Vince Piggins and his COPO program.

Don Yenko typified this breed. Yenko owned Yenko Chevrolet, a Chevy dealership in Canonsburg, Pennsylvania, just outside of Pittsburgh. He was a life-long hot rodder and had achieved some success as a drag racer. In 1967, Yenko removed the engines from 54

With a hood filched from a 1967 Corvette and enough exterior badging to raise the interest of any law enforcement within a three-county radius, the '67 Yenko Camaro was stupid fast. In the real world, it generated upwards of 450 horsepower.

In an effort to keep down weight and minimize distractions, the interior of the 1967 Yenko Camaro was rather plain. Note the huge tachometer hiding the instrument panel; during a drag race, monitoring engine revs was all important.

SS350 Camaros and replaced them with the L72 version of Chevy's 427 V-8. The L72 featured forged aluminum pistons, forged crankshaft journals, and four-bolt main bearing caps. Mechanical lifters helped the car develop 425 horsepower and 460 lb-ft of torque, but they also meant that the owner would have to deal with valve-lash adjustments.

Those sold well, so in 1968, he performed the same transplant on another 64 Camaro SS396s. Again, these cars sold well, but transplanting the engine required a lot of work and expense. Plus, there was the problem of unwanted leftover stock engines. For 1969, Yenko approached Chevrolet about forming a partnership in building 427-cubic-inch Camaros and Chevelles and selling them around the country. He convinced Chevrolet that he could sell 500 cars—enough to earn both Yenko and Chevrolet a profit.

Having seen the success Oldsmobile had with the Hurst/Olds, Chevrolet took Yenko up on his offer. Yenko ordered a run of COPO 9561 Camaros, meaning cars fitted with the L72 version of Chevrolet's 427-cubic-inch V-8. This engine had 11.0:1 compression pistons pumping up and down in its cast-iron block, and a solid-lifter camshaft opened the big-port valves in its cast-iron heads. The combination was good for 450 horsepower in 1969. When spinning a 4.10:1 Posi-Traction rear end through an M21 four-speed transmission, the Yenko version of the L72 could propel the stock Y/SC (Yenko Super Car) Camaro through the quarter-mile in the 12-second range. Yenko sold 199 such Camaros in 1969.

continued on page 128

In an effort to reduce weight and feed cool air to the engine compartment, a fiberglass hood was fitted to the 1968 Yenko Camaro. Only seven were made with L72 V-8s; most used 396-cubic-inch engines.

Because a 396-cubic-inch engine just isn't enough in a 1968 Yenko Camaro, the original owner sprang for a 427 rat engine. Yenko dressed up his creations more than most aftermarket enhancers tended to, fitting Yenko wheel centers and Yenko badging anywhere he could, including the glove box door.

Don Yenko was well connected within Chevrolet, and he was able to get his hands on a supply of L72 427-cubic-inch engines. Developed to propel Corvettes, they were rated at 450 horsepower in the first part of 1968. Finally, truth in advertising.

The 1968 Yenko Camaros used Super Sport underpinnings; thus, they came with the SS bumblebee stripe. Not stock was the fiberglass hood, complete with huge functional scoops. Big-block engines tend to need lots of fresh air.

Above: When Don Yenko's technicians fitted out this 1968 Camaro with a 427-cubic-inch engine, a Hurst race shifter was needed to funnel the power through the four-speed transmission. With its current gearing, it's been calculated that this vehicle is capable of reaching 183 miles per hour.

Right: Due to General Motors' policy limiting performance cars to 400-cubic-inch engines during the 1960s, the enterprising and well-connected Don Yenko built his own big-inch Chevrolet muscle cars, like this 427 Camaro.

Yenko wasn't shy about plastering his logo anywhere he could, including on the headrests on a 1969 427 Camaro. Whatever it took to get noticed.

Some Chevrolet dealers, like Don Yenko of Canonsburg, Pennsylvania, used the COPO program to install huge engines in cars like the Camaro and Chevelle, creating more-muscular muscle cars. You can never have too much muscle under the hood.

Chicago dealers John and Edward Stephani of Nickey Chevrolet wanted their dealership to be known as a go-to destination for buyers wanting break-neck acceleration. Nickey teamed up with Anaheim, California, racer Bill Thomas to build street-legal drag cars, stuffed with 427 cubic inches and a lot of attitude.

continued from page 119

Other Chevrolet dealers around the country took it upon themselves to create a Bowtie response to the big-inch Mustangs stealing the Camaro's thunder. Dana Chevrolet of South Gate, California, was one such dealership, exploiting the COPO program to produce an L72-powered Camaro that out-muscled the 355-horsepower engine in the Shelby GT500. *Car Life* turned a 14.2-second quarter-mile with the Dana 427 Camaro tested for the magazine's April 1967 issue.

Chicago's Nickey Chevrolet also sold a dealer-special L72-powered Camaro. Most of the production work on the Nickey Camaros was done at Bill Thomas Race Cars of Anaheim, California. *Car and Driver* tested a Nickey/Thomas Camaro 427 for its September 1967 issue and turned a 13.9-second quarter-mile.

Neither the Dana nor the Nickey Camaros were inexpensive. The base price for a Dana was $4,495, and the example *Car Life* tested retailed for $5,500, including the cost of all the options: RS appearance package, vinyl roof, custom interior, tinted glass, radio, appearance and light groups, power disc brakes, and Traction Master traction bars. The Nickey car topped out even higher at $5,922, but it had some serious and heavy-duty drag racing parts, like an explosion-proof bell housing and competition clutch and flywheel. These cars weren't cheap to run, either; the Nickey car, with which *Car and Driver* got between 7 and 10 miles per gallon, could only cover between 130 and 185 miles between fill ups.

continued on page 134

Deep pockets were needed to get behind the wheel of a 1967 Stage III Nickey Camaro, which cost $1,089 over MSRP. The resulting package was loaded with special induction and exhaust systems, a competition ring and pinion gear set, M & H Racemaster tires at the rear, and a score of other go-fast parts.

In 1967, the emphasis was on acceleration, not braking. Thus, you saw drum brakes hiding behind the Torq-Thrust wheels that Nickey Chevrolet fitted on its brutal 427-cubic-inch Camaros.

This 1967 Nickey Camaro had plenty of flash, from the vibrant paint to the redline tires on Cragar S/S wheels. Yet with a 427-cubic-inch engine sourced from a Corvette, it could humiliate virtually any other purpose-built, street-legal drag car.

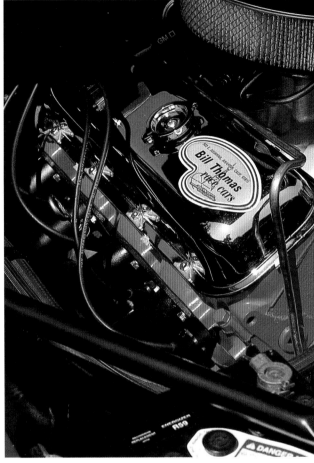

Just your regular, race-prepared 427-cubic-inch V-8. In a vehicle as light as a Camaro, the biggest problem a driver had was getting the 450-plus horsepower to the ground. Bill Thomas was known for his wicked-fast Cheetah race car.

Some people might comment on the front end of the 1967 Nickey 427 Camaro sitting higher than a stock Camaro. When a vehicle is set up for the drag strip, weight transfer is all important, and nonstock springs were required to maximize performance. At rest, they tended to raise the nose of the car.

Left: With the exception of a few exterior badges, 1967 Nickey Camaro owners found that their money bought what was under the skin. From a scattershield to a traction kit, these cars were turnkey racers.

Above: A simple decal was all that Nickey Chevrolet put on its regular street cars, and the monstrous rat-engined Camaros wore it as well. Quite a few Chicagoans saw this view of the 1967 Camaro. It was prudent to race with less than half a tank of fuel, as under hard acceleration, gas could slam against the filler cap.

Surely there's a gas station nearby. With a 500-horsepower, L88 427-cubic-inch monster under the hood, this 1968 Baldwin-Motion Camaro travels very short distances between fill-ups. It could cover the drag strip in 11.50 seconds at 120 miles per hour—on period tires.

continued from page 129

Baldwin-Motion Performance Group took the dealer-special concept a step further, selling super-high-performance cars that, like today's tuner-car builders, they built themselves instead of relying on the COPO program. Formed in 1967 by Joel Rosen and Marty Schorr from Motion Performance, a New York–based speed shop that specialized in Chevrolet products, and Baldwin Chevrolet parts manager John Mahler in Baldwin, New York (a New York City suburb), Baldwin-Motion built the Camaros that many buyers really wanted.

Baldwin-Motion offered two versions of its Camaro: an SS that featured a 425-horsepower 427-cubic-inch L72, and Phase III cars, which featured engines starting at 500 horsepower and climbing as far as owners' imaginations, pocketbooks, and courage would take them. They built each car to order, and every Phase III Camaro was guaranteed to run through the quarter-mile in no more than 11.5 seconds.

To achieve such remarkable performance, Motion Performance resorted to every speed trick at its disposal when building a Phase III car. After pulling the stock 396 and mounting an L72 427, a buyer could choose from 38 different performance options. Prices started at $3,795, which included the brand-new Camaro. When Phase III was selected, prices started at $4,998 and went up from there, depending on just how fast an owner wanted to go. To help keep costs down, Motion Performance crated up and resold the 396 engines for $595.

continued on page 140

Joel Rosen, founder of Motion Performance, felt that people should notice his creations at rest as well as at speed. Cragar S/S wheels were the street racer's choice in the late 1960s.

Above: Chevrolet rated the L88 engine at 430 horsepower, when in fact it made well over 500. Boasting a compression ratio of 12.5:1, it breathed through a three-barrel, 950-cfm carburetor.

Right: Only two Phase III Baldwin-Motion Camaros were built in 1968. To help in launching at the drag strip, the battery was mounted in the trunk, as were steel weights. The 1967 Corvette-style hood was essentially for show, but it did look good.

Left: Absolutely nothing on the street in 1968 was faster than a Baldwin-Motion Camaro. Baldwin-Motion offered two versions of its Camaro: an SS that featured a 425-horsepower 427-cubic-inch L72; and Phase III cars, which featured engines starting at 500 horsepower and climbing from there.

Above: Replacement Stewart-Warner gauges filled the instrument panel of the 1968 Phase III Baldwin-Motion Camaro. Being able to monitor the condition of the race engine beneath the fiberglass Stinger hood could mean the difference between a win and a ride home on a hook.

It was a very rare day that a competitor to the 1968 Phase III Baldwin-Motion L88 Camaro saw anything except this view of the car. Joel Rosen kept the black plate between the taillights that came stock on SS 396 Camaros.

continued from page 135

In his book, *Muscle Car Confidential* (one of the most entertaining muscle car books ever published), author Joe Oldham describes driving his personal Baldwin-Motion SS-427:

The best run was on the Connecting against a guy with a big mouth and a Hemi-powered '68 Road Runner. He was the self-proclaimed "King of the Connecting" and his "worked" Hemi had never been beaten by any stock-bodied car—until he met the Chevrolet gods that night, and the "SS-427" emblem on my trunk lid.

What was even better than street racing in this car was just cruising. The head-turning ability of the car was incredible, even better than the Viper when it first appeared. Everybody looked. It was something special. It had that hairy, menacing look that said, "Hey, don't fuck with me or I'll blow your fucking doors off." Yes, driving the car was definitely an ego trip . . . .

Of all the cars I have ever owned, this is the one I most regret not having today. Not because they sell for hundreds of thousands at the Barrett-Jackson auctions, but because this was the coolest car I ever owned—and maybe the coolest car I ever drove.

COPO 9560

Piggins had an even grander vision for the Camaro. Piggins had the Camaro, and he had the aluminum ZL-1 engine. Installing the mighty ZL-1 engine in the Camaro would make it a Mustang-stomper, but there was no way corporate brass would allow such a reprehensible act. Not only would it make Ralph Nader and his cronies apoplectic, it would not result in a very good street car. The engine had never been developed for street use and lacked such amenities as a choke. It had never been designed to use with a restrictive street exhaust system, and the open-plenum manifold meant it would be all but impossible to drive on the street.

Mounting a ZL-1 engine in the lightweight Camaro body presented problems of the corporate-political variety, but the actual swap was a simple bolt-in proposition. While corporate management would never approve, the idea was just too cool not to try it. The engine was given COPO code 9560 for Camaro use and offered through

continued on page 145

Rare, subtle, and stupid fast, the 1969 Camaro ZL-1 used an all-aluminum 427-cubic-inch race engine to humiliate everyone else on the street. It was designed to dominate the NHRA's Super Stock C and D classes, but the NHRA ruled the car ineligible for Super Stock racing, forcing it to compete in the F/X class, where it raced against all-out Funny Cars.

Right: Model year 1969 embraced big numbers, and this trio on the hood of a Camaro could only mean trouble for the car in the other lane. The aluminum V-8 utilized a functional cowl-induction system to ingest fresh air.

Below: COPO 9560AA was corporate speak for a 1969 ZL-1 Camaro. With open headers, the engine would dyno at 575 horsepower, yet Chevrolet rated it at 430. Insurance companies were starting to cast an eye toward muscle cars, so GM felt that discretion might be a prudent course of action.

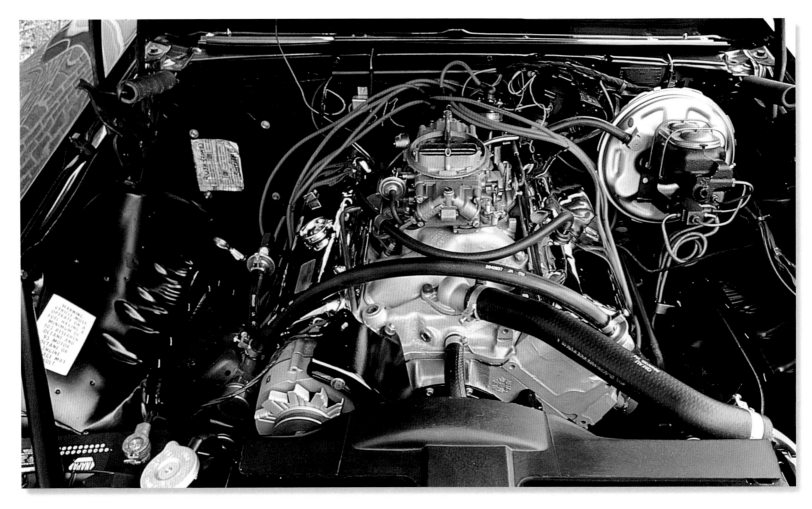

Above: Chevrolet kept the exterior of the 1969 ZL-1 Camaro under the radar, eschewing fancy wheels for lightweight and cheap dog-dish hubcaps. With the true purpose of the ZL-1 being race duty, it was a given that most owners would replace the factory rolling stock with something bigger and stickier.

Left: All of the '69 ZL-1 Camaros were built at the Norwood, Ohio, plant between December 1968 and June 1969. For all its power and ferocity, the ZL-1 was street-legal in all 50 states.

Above: Many consider the 1969 model year's styling the pinnacle of Camaro design. Stuff an all-aluminum ZL-1 engine under the hood, and you can add rarity to the equation. The small chin spoiler was an early attempt at introducing aerodynamic aids to street car design.

Right: At first glance, the 1969 Camaro ZL-1 might be mistaken for a six-cylinder economy car. The breakdown on production was 47 manual transmission–equipped cars and 22 automatics. A good-running ZL-1 is actually an easy car to drive; what's not so easy is keeping your right foot out of the big carburetor.

Chevrolet increased the angle of the grille's V for the 1969 model year, creating a more aggressive front end. The full-width grille opening allowed plenty of air to flow into the radiator, which, in the case of this ZL-1 Camaro, was a very good thing.

continued from page 141

Piggins' back-room program. If someone was brave enough or foolhardy enough to plunk down an extra $4,160 over the base price of the Camaro and request COPO option 9560, he received a ZL-1 engine with a Z/28 body wrapped around it, including the Z/28's racing suspension, but without the Z/28 stripes. The cars featured street mufflers, which robbed the awe-inspiring engine of a bit of its thunder, but not enough to tame it. Even with its restrictive exhaust system, the car possessed enough snort to make a trip to the grocery store a genuinely terrifying experience. Chevrolet hoped the high price of the ZL-1 engine would be enough to keep people from buying the car for anything but racing use.

Chevrolet produced an estimated 69 of these outlandish cars, none of which made their mark at the drag strip. It wasn't because the cars were slow; a well-tuned ZL-1 Camaro could easily break into the 10-second bracket. The problem was the competition. Chevrolet rated ZL-1 horsepower at a ridiculously low 425 ponies so it could compete in Super Stock C and D classes, but the sanctioning bodies saw through this cheap ploy and classified it as a modified, where it would have to run against purpose-built race cars. By that time, the F/X class had morphed into the Funny Car classes, and the 10-second ZL-1 Camaro found itself racing against all-out dragsters running through the quarter-mile traps in the 7-second bracket.

Released to legalize Chevrolet's involvement in the SCCA Trans Am racing series, the Z/28 was a serious road racing machine that you could drive on the street. The combination of a lightweight, high-revving V-8 in a Camaro with a race-bred suspension resulted in a legendary car in its own day.

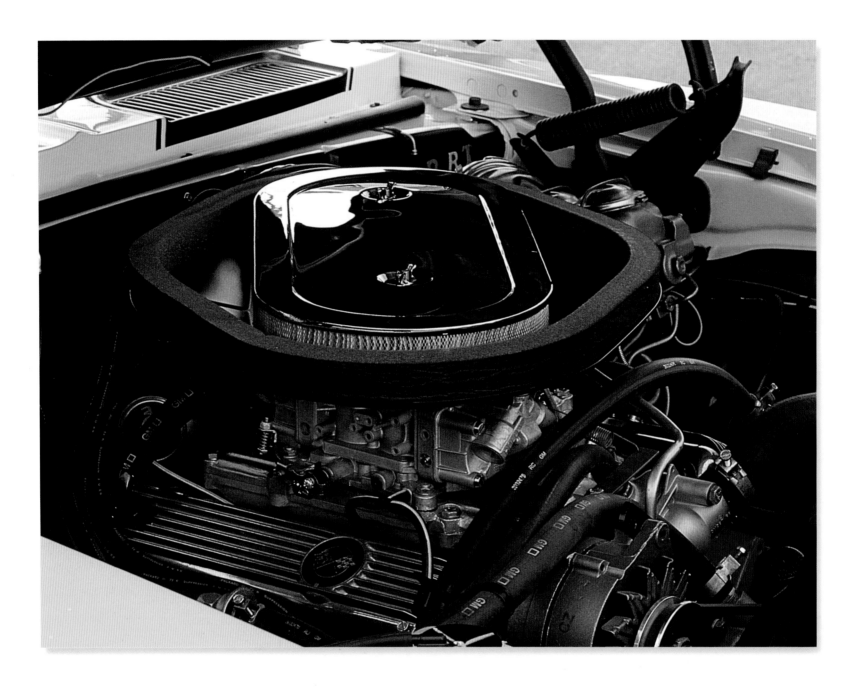

Designed to allow the 302-cubic-inch V-8 to run at sustained high speeds, the Z/28 Cross-Ram intake manifold used a pair of four-barrel carburetors to supply the race-bred engine with enough fuel at speed.

Camaro Version 1.2

The 1969 Camaro body in which Vince Piggins mounted the ZL-1 engine had received enough changes and improvements to qualify as a nearly new model: version 1.2, if you will.

Given that the Camaro was due to be redesigned for the 1970 model year, most observers were, if not shocked, pretty darned surprised by the degree of change in the 1969 version. Subtle styling changes led to a car that was lower, wider, and more muscular-looking than earlier cars. The reshaped body panels on the doors, fenders, quarter panels, and front and rear valences added an aggressive attitude to the 1969 cars. Designers abandoned the fluid Coke-bottle curves over the fenders and flattened

Drawing cool, ambient air from the high-pressure area at the base of the windshield, the 1969 Z/28 utilized an optional hood with special ducting on the underside to direct outside air directly onto the air cleaner in an effort to boost horsepower.

Chevrolet mounted the 1969 Z/28's auxiliary engine gauges at the forward end of the center console.

Hound's-tooth upholstery added a bit of visual style to the basically Spartan interior of the 1969 Z/28. Like all good sports cars, the purpose of the vehicle was to perform well in all three arenas—acceleration, braking, and handling—and the Z/28 was highly competent in each area.

the wheelwell arches, smoothing the profile and giving the car a more purposeful stance. Fake vents resembling sharklike gills in front of the rear tires gave the car a menacing, predatory look. The car was still obviously the same Camaro it had been for the previous two years, but it had a completely different presence.

That difference continued inside the cab, too. The changes weren't revolutionary—the main change was the addition of a new instrument panel—but the overall detail changes and improvements in comfort and convenience gave the car a very different feel. Inside and out, the 1969 Camaro was harder-edged and more masculine than the earlier cars.

The styling changes became even more dramatic if the buyer ordered the Rally Sport styling package. RS-equipped Camaros featured thin stripes that accentuated the striking new character lines in the sheet metal, along with other detail changes, but the most obvious

change in the RS package was the new grille. A pair of doors still covered the headlights, and they still retracted behind the center portion of the grille, but instead of solid black doors that visually blended into the main portion of the grille, these were now body-colored panels with three slotted windows in each panel. In theory, this allowed the lights to shine through even if the doors failed, which was a fairly common occurrence, but in reality, this system didn't allow a useful amount of light to shine through a stuck door. In an attempt to make stuck headlight doors a less common occurrence, Chevy designers had switched from electrical motors to vacuum-operated servo motors for opening and closing the doors during the 1968 model year. They also included pumps to squirt cleaning fluid onto the lights as part of the RS package but discovered that, without wiper blades to scrape off the wet headlights, the washers weren't terribly effective; this was a one-year-only feature.

Only 311 1969 Camaros were fitted with the $710.95 L89 option with the 375-horsepower, 396-cubic-inch V-8 aluminum heads.

The RS option cost $131.65, while the SS equipment package went for $327.55. As in prior years, the SS badging took precedence over the RS badging.

With the iron-block 396-cubic-inch engine over the front wheels, the 1969 Camaro SS couldn't handle the twisties as well as its Z/28 cousin, but the big-block Camaro was meant to accelerate briskly in a straight line.

Substantial changes also lurked in the chassis and under the hood. The six-cylinder engines received no changes from the previous year. These engines found homes in a fairly small percentage of Camaros in 1969. Of the two six-cylinders, 17,588 buyers opted for the base 140-horsepower, 230-cubic-inch version while 18,660 popped for the 155-horsepower, 250-cubic-inch unit, a $26.35 option.

In 1969, performance ruled the American marketplace, as evidenced by the fact that more people were willing to shell out $458.15 for the Z/28's 302-cubic-inch V-8—20,302 of them, to be exact—than selected either of the economy six-cylinder engines.

The Z/28's 302 was better than ever for 1969. Chevy engineers had strengthened the forged crankshaft and connecting rods the previous year in an attempt to withstand the demands placed on the engine in Trans-Am racing and had given the main-bearing caps of the three middle journals the same stiff four-bolt design as the outer main-bearing caps, making this the strongest, stiffest, small-block V-8 Chevrolet had built up until that time. For 1969, they made further detail improvements, such as a strengthened accessory drive system able to withstand the stratospheric revs at which this overachieving engine thrived. The Z/28 also received an optional fresh-air hood system—"cowl

Dover White with Hugger Orange stripes, the 1969 Camaro pace car was popular, with 3,674 sold. Engine choices ranged from 300 to 375 horsepower.

Mandatory options included D80 spoiler equipment, Z22 Rally Sport package, ZL2 air induction hood, and Z11 Indy sport convertible accents.

Jim Rathmann, winner of the 1960 Indianapolis 500, drove the actual pace car on May 30, 1969. This was the Camaro's second appearance at the Greatest Spectacle in Racing.

induction," in Chevy-speak—coded ZL2. This $79 option was required when ordering one of the COPO big-block cars.

At the beginning of 1969 production, the base engine was the same 327-cubic-inch V-8 it had always been, though now rated at 217 horsepower in two-barrel form. But midway through the model year, Chevrolet began offering a new 307-cubic-inch, 210-horsepower engine as the base unit. This engine had the same stroke as the 327 but featured smaller cylinder bores to achieve its smaller displacement. Chevy engineers did this in an attempt to create a more fuel-efficient engine, but any increased miserliness was more theoretical than real. The only tangible result of the 20-cubic-inch displacement decrease was an engine with a bore-and-stroke ratio

uniquely unsuited for high-performance driving; over the years, the 307 has earned a reputation as being the most unloved engine in the pantheon of Chevy small-blocks.

Midway through the model year, Chevrolet dropped all versions of the 327 and the 225 horsepower LM1 350-cubic-inch engine, making the 250-horsepower L65 version of the 350 the next step up the Camaro performance ladder. The L48 350 gained 5 horsepower for 1969, jumping to 300 ponies, making it officially the strongest small-block, though the 302 still packed all those hidden horsepower for anyone willing to rev the snot out of the engine. The 396-cubic-inch big-blocks available in the SS396—325-horsepower L35, 350-horsepower L34, 375-horsepower L78, and the aluminum-head L89, also generating 375 horsepower—remained virtually

Pace car replicas used the mandatory Z87 orange hound's-tooth upholstery.

unchanged, with some minor tweaks such as improved water pumps and accessory drive systems.

Transmission offerings stayed the same, except for a clerical change in the codes for the standard three-speed manual transmission that hardly anyone bought anyway, but Chevrolet instituted a major change in the shifter for the optional four-speed units; Chevrolet finally abandoned the Muncie shifter and linkage, which every Camaro road test ever published had described as awful or worse, and adopted a much-improved Hurst shifter and linkage setup.

JL8

Under the skin, the chassis was almost identical to earlier cars, except where it needed to be modified to accept the reshaped sheet metal. Suspension changes too were kept to a minimum, consisting primarily of revalved shocks and recalibrated spring rates. Chevrolet offered an optional 1-inch-diameter front stabilizer bar, which had been

Automatic-equipped Indianapolis 500 pace car replicas in 1969 used the durable Turbo Hydra-matic three-speed transmission. The floor-mounted shifter was a $10.55 option.

developed for COPO 9737. Called the Sports Car Conversion option, COPO 9737 was a suspension kit for serious racers.

The most radical option offered outside of the COPO program came about as a result of the developmental work done for the Donahue/Penske Trans-Am racing effort. For the first time, Camaro buyers could order RPO JL8—four-wheel disc brakes. Intended as an option for serious racers, RPO JL8 carried a serious price: $500.50. To ensure on-track durability, each JL8 rear axle assembly was shot-peened and Magnafluxed.

For buyers not wanting to shell out $500, dealers also offered the JL8 Service Package, a rear-disc braking system available from the parts counter. These are much more common but differ from the factory setup in a couple of notable ways. The rear axle

tube of the factory JL8 cars are tapered at the ends, whereas cars with added-on JL8 brakes have the same axle tubes as drum brake cars, without the tapered ends. Chevrolet engineers also gave factory JL8 cars larger-diameter front brake rotors: 11.75 inches versus 11 inches. Factory JL8-equipped Z/28s are among the rarest (and most valuable) of all Camaros today.

Indianapolis Pace Car, V2.1

Once again, the Camaro was selected to pace the Indianapolis 500. The pace car, a 1969 L78-powered Dover White RS/SS396 convertible with Hugger Orange stripes, would be driven by 1960 Indy winner Jim Rathmann. In addition to the customary 100 similar cars provided for use during the race weekend, Chevrolet gave a car to that year's race winner (Mario Andretti). Best of all, the division planned to build replicas to sell to the general public. These replica cars came in the same white-orange color combination as the pace car, along with the distinctive orange-and-black hound's-tooth interior.

Chevrolet built a limited quantity—3,675—convertibles with the pace car replica option. Not all dealers were offered the car, and those that were had to preorder the exact number they wanted, all of which conspired to keep production numbers for this popular car below 3,700 units. Coded RPO Z11, this $36.90 trim package turned out to be one of the best investments a Camaro buyer lucky enough to purchase an example could make; that initial investment of under $40 would net an owner an additional 20–25 percent over a comparably equipped 1969 convertible in similar condition if he or she was selling the car today. Even more valuable are the small number of pace car replica coupes. No production numbers are available for these cars, coded RPO Z10, and they change hands so infrequently that most price guides don't list their value, but it's probably somewhere north of "if you have to ask . . ." When shopping for a pace car replica, however, a potential buyer needs to be especially wary. Not all RS/SS convertibles with the Dover White-Hugger Orange paint scheme are genuine Z11 cars, and virtually none of the coupes in that color combination are Z10 cars. Before paying a premium for an Indy pace car, a buyer should see documented proof that the car is what it purports to be. In this case, the buyer needs to be-more-than-ware; he or she needs to be paranoid.

The year 1969 marked a high point for the Camaro. After getting off to a slow start in the Trans-Am series (Ford won four of the first five races with its highly competitive Boss 302), the Donahue/Penske team won six of the last seven races, once again winning a driver's championship and helping Chevrolet win its second consecutive manufacturer's title. The 1969 street cars proved the most popular yet, selling 243,085 units, a record that would stand until 1978. For the first time, the Camaro was nipping at the hooves of the Mustang, which sold just 299,824 units in 1969. Many Camaro fans consider the 1969 version one of the best and most desirable Camaros ever built, a car that ended the decade on a very high note for Chevrolet.

Opposite: Unlike the standard blacked-out rear panel treatment found on SS Camaros, 1969 Indianapolis 500 pace car replicas used a Dover White body-color panel.

CHAPTER THREE

THE EUROPEAN CAMARO

The Camaro adopted a more European look with the 1970 1/2 model. Wind tunnel research showed that the front chin and rear wing spoilers generated usable downforce, ideal for a vehicle with the performance potential of the Z28.

Even though the Camaro had its best year yet in 1969, anyone who followed the auto industry closely understood that the Chevrolet faced some serious challenges, as did the U.S. auto industry in general. The future looked particularly bleak for sporty, youth-oriented cars like Chevrolet's Camaro. On the surface, sales were strong, but they were also misleading. An extended 17-month production period inflated 1969 numbers. While Chevrolet technically sold 243,085 1969 Camaros, the division only sold 159,201 Camaros during calendar year 1969, and only 193,986 1969 model-year Camaros between the fall 1968 introduction and January 1, 1970. Chevrolet sold the remaining 49,099 1969 Camaros in the first months of 1970, while the division readied an all-new car to be released in the spring of 1970. Camaros continued to sell, but not at previous rates, and often not for full retail price, hammering Chevrolet's profit margins. As *Hot Rod* magazine noted in its October 1969 issue, "Now would be a perfect time to cut the price down on the '69-appearing Camaro."

Above: There was no small amount of anguish and worry about the vulnerability of the dramatic nose. At the time, GM officials demanded that the vehicle withstand an in-house one-and-a-half mile-per-hour barrier test, which showed that the pretty arrangement could not be used as the standard front end, but rules were bent to allow the stunning (and delicate) front end design to survive as part of the optional RS package.

Left: GM executives were nervous about the radical design of the second-generation Z28, but when it hit showrooms in early 1970, the public was overjoyed.

Before the public saw the car, GM styling czar Bill Mitchell showed the new Camaro to close friend and Grand Prix race driver Sterling Moss to gauge his reaction. Moss was stunned when he saw the full-size fiberglass models, asking Mitchell if this design was going to be sold as a Chevrolet. When Mitchell answered in the affirmative, Moss was very pleased.

Chevrolet began developing a replacement for the Camaro as soon as the 1967 model had been officially announced. Chevrolet's management was tired of having the Camaro play second fiddle to the Mustang and intended to make the next-generation Camaro a truly world-class car, one that wouldn't suffer from the rushed development of the original. The new Camaro would not borrow suspension bits from lowly economy sedans; it would be the closest thing to a four-seat sports car that Chevrolet could build.

In addition to creating the best-handling American car available, Chevrolet's designers intended to create the best-looking American car. GM Design Vice President Bill Mitchell oversaw the styling of the car personally. Mitchell's designers looked to Italian sports cars for inspiration, particularly the Ferraris of the 1960s. Mitchell

encouraged his staff to make the car as exciting as possible, unconstrained by the same restrictions applied to normal passenger cars. He did not want anyone to confuse the Camaro with a Nova or a Chevelle.

Chevrolet's styling staff performed exactly as Mitchell demanded, creating a stunningly beautiful design that could have come from Maranello, Italy, as easily as it came from Detroit. But this design required GM's engineering staff to come up with all sorts of creative ways to turn the concept into a production car. The stylish front end, long doors, large side windows, and overall packaging kept engineers working long hours figuring out how to meet all federal regulations and how to actually mass produce this exotic new automobile on an assembly line.

With its aggressive stance and Hugger Orange paint with dual white stripes, the 1970 Z28 was hard to miss. Fortunately, it could walk the walk. The Z28 option cost $572.95.

GM management decided to delay the introduction from the traditional fall 1969 period and wait until February 1970 to solve the problems of mass producing such a complex car design, and to give the Chevrolet design staff the time they needed to make the car as close to perfect as possible. The car debuted on Friday, February 13, 1970. Apparently Chevrolet management wasn't superstitious, but the events of the coming years may well have made them so.

"A Sports Car for the Four of You"

Chevrolet offered the 1970 1/2 Camaro in the same iterations as the previous generation: Sport Coupe, Super Sport, and Z28 (the slash disappeared from the badge on the new car), with the Rally Sport trim package once again being made available. Where non-RS Camaros featured a thin chrome bumper across the front of the grille, cars with the RS package had a urethane band extending around the central grille, with short chrome bumpers on either side. It may not have been the most durable arrangement in the event of parallel-parking mishaps, but it was stunningly beautiful . . . as was the rest of the car.

The May 1970 issue of *Car and Driver* described a Z28 it tested as: "a finely drawn shape, free of Detroit's customary visual trickery." *Motorcade* magazine summed it up a bit differently in its May 1970 issue, saying that Chevrolet designers wanted the Camaro to be "more than a kiss-yer-sister kind of car." Designers clearly hit their mark when aiming for European style, as evidenced from the pages of the August 1970 issue of *Road Test* magazine: "From the rear view, the new Camaro looks like an Italian GT. The smooth lines are classic, and only the rumble from the twin exhausts reminds one of its Michigan blood lines."

Chevrolet's advertising agency made good use of the new Camaro's stylish appearance, running ads in major magazines describing the car as "a sports car for the four of you." But it wasn't all hype; for the moment at least, the new Camaro had the hardware to back up the advertisers' claims.

Considerable effort was expended by the engineering staff to design a functional and affordable rear spoiler. This particular example has generated some controversy, and is believed to be a prototype 1971 spoiler.

The 1970 Camaro's designers placed the driver as close to the center of the wheelbase as possible, as seen on this Chevrolet line drawing. Classic pony car proportions are evident in the side view; the long hood/short deck gave the vehicle an aggressive stance. *General Motors Corp. Used with permission, GM Media Archives*

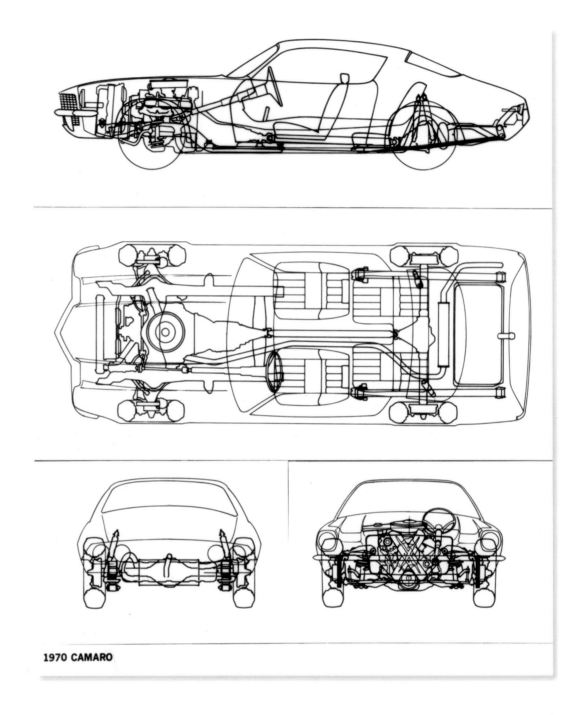

1970 CAMARO

For 1970, Chevrolet offered the most powerful RPO engines yet, a necessary change due to a fairly substantial increase in curb weight. The 1969 SS396 Camaro had weighed 3,490 pounds; the 1970 SS396 weighed in at a portly 3,850 pounds. Because of this weight gain, the base 140-horsepower six was dropped from the lineup, leaving the 155-horsepower version as the sole six-cylinder offering for the tight-fisted Camaro buyer. A buyer with slightly looser purse strings could splurge and spend the $90 needed to upgrade to the 307-cubic-inch V-8 engine, now rated at 200 horsepower. Another $31.60 would net the buyer the 250-horsepower, two-barrel version of the 350-cubic-inch

This cutaway 1971 Camaro was one of several Chevy Shows and Exhibits displays that traveled to auto shows and dealerships. Here it helps draw traffic to Dick Genthe Cheverolet in Southgate, Michigan. *General Motors Corp. Used with permission, GM Media Archives*

engine, but the real enthusiast started with the 300-horsepower four-barrel L48 350 and went up from there.

The 302 disappeared from the lineup in 1970. Rule changes in SCCA racing meant that Chevrolet no longer had to build a 5-liter version of its engine to homologate the car for the Trans-Am series. Not that it mattered much anymore; the Donahue/Penske team split with Chevrolet after the 1969 season and went to work for American Motors. Before a Camaro would win another Trans-Am championship, John Lennon would be dead, Ronald Reagan would be president, and production Camaros would be fuel-injected.

In 1970, ordering RPO Z28 meant getting the highly tuned LT-1 350-cubic-inch engine from the Corvette. The LT-1 featured all of the performance parts that had made the 302 such a fast, durable engine: four-bolt mains, forged-steel crankshaft, 11.0:1 pistons, aluminum intake, 780-cfm Holley carburetor, and a steep, solid-lifter

Long and lithe, the 1970 Camaro equipped with an RS appearance package offered a gaping grille and tiny corner front bumpers. Non-RS Camaros featured a full-width front bumper. *General Motors Corp. Used with permission, GM Media Archives*

camshaft. In the Corvette, the engine produced 370 horsepower; in the Camaro, that number was down to 360 because of a more restrictive exhaust system.

In Camaro tune, the LT-1 generated 370 lb-ft of torque, making the new Z28 one of the quickest Z28s yet. *Car and Driver*, which tended to be less aggressive at the drag strip than drag racing-oriented magazines like *Hot Rod*, recorded a 14.2-second quarter-mile in its May 1970 Z28 road test.

The Z28 package cost $572.95 in 1970—quite a jump in price—but in addition to the LT-1 engine, the money included the excellent F41 sport suspension package, normally a $30.55 option, along with heavy-duty springs front and rear, sexy 15x7-inch styled wheels shod with F60 bias-ply steel-belted tires, heavy-duty radiator, engine chrome package, dual exhaust, rear deck spoiler, and special stripes.

When Is a 396 Not a 396?

Chevrolet once again offered the SS396 version of the Camaro for 1970 in both L34 and L78 versions. Even though horsepower and torque ratings remained identical— 350 horsepower and 415 lb-ft of torque for the L34, and 375 horsepower and 415 lb-ft

Stylists in Studio Three experimented with wheel spats on the 1970 Camaro in an effort to improve the look of the Chevy pony car as well as the aerodynamics. Other areas that received attention were front chin and rear spoilers. *General Motors Corp. Used with permission, GM Media Archives*

of torque for the L78—the 396 engines were different from the previous year, mainly in that they were not 396-cubic-inch engines.

For 1970, Chevrolet engineers bored out the 396 engine, taking the bore from 4.094 inches to 4.126 inches in an attempt to retain the power drained from the engine by increased pollution-control equipment and by consumer trends toward more power-robbing luxury items like air conditioning, power steering, and automatic transmissions.

Even though the trend toward larger numbers usually meant more sales, Chevrolet's marketing folks decided that the name "402" didn't have the panache of "396." "SS396" sounded like a badass American street fighter; "SS402" sounded like some front-wheel-drive French car with an air-bladder suspension.

The press lavished praise on the new Camaros as never before. *Car and Driver* wrote of the new Z28: "There is nothing precious about the Camaro Z/28 [the magazine

The stylists in Studio Two were fine-tuning the 1970 1/2 Camaro design, but a number of items on this clay mockup did not see production, including the script inboard of the driver-side headlight and the lower outboard openings. On the production vehicle, the turn signals would fill those spaces. *General Motors Corp. Used with permission, GM Media Archives*

continued to use the slash even though GM had abandoned it]. Chevrolet will stamp them out like the government does cupro-nickel quarters, but it is an automobile of uncommon merit."

Magazines especially praised the new car's handling characteristics. Chevrolet had engineered the car to have higher-effort steering gears with a variable ratio so that the ratio was quicker toward the end of the wheel's turn and slowed up as the wheel approached center. This kept the steering quick without being twitchy. They also relocated the steering linkage ahead of the ball joints, which freed up room for a more sophisticated front suspension. *Car and Driver* wrote: "The result of these two developments is a car of exceptional handling—probably the best Detroit has ever produced."

At first glance, this 1970 Camaro appears stock, but this vehicle was a test car for a lifting-door design later seen on the four-rotor Corvette in 1973. Economics kept the door from becoming a production reality. *General Motors Corp. Used with permission, GM Media Archives*

Sometimes prototype parts never see production, and the lift-door concept was one of these. Installed on a 1970 Camaro, it's evident that the door would not have been cost-effective. *General Motors Corp. Used with permission, GM Media Archives*

Chevrolet engineers pulled the engine back in the structure to allow room for an effective air conditioning system, but by doing that, and leaving the wheelbase the same, rear seat room suffered.

Even *Road & Track*, a magazine that generally preferred European sports cars to Detroit iron, praised the new Camaro's handling when it tested an SS350 for its May 1970 issue, writing that the variable-ratio steering gear "gives a degree of natural steering heretofore unknown in domestic power steering. In fact, it's quite close to being as good as our ideal (the Mercedes-Benz device) and the quick, variable ratio makes the Camaro uncommonly maneuverable for such a long-hooded beast.

"In fact, we'll have to say it's the best American car we've ever driven, and more importantly, it's one of the most satisfying cars for all-around use we've ever driven."

When *Road Test* evaluated a Camaro SS396 for its August 1970 issue, it wrote: "The car is a responsive machine, makes wonderful noises, causes small boys to whistle, and

One of Chevy's most popular engines was the LT-1. In the Z28 Camaro, the LT-1 generated 370 lb-ft of torque and 360 SAE gross horsepower.

causes gas-station attendants to wash all the windows. Yes, folks, we think the 1970 Camaro with SS options is the neatest thing we have ever driven from Detroit's mass production lines."

The praise was universal. *Motorcade* magazine, which despised testing what it called "squishy pieces of Dee-troit pig iron," loved the new Camaro, saying the Z28 possessed "the essence of road feel through taut suspension and positive steering . . . The Camaro will do everything a Jag will do, and about 30 percent quicker, surer, and faster." Of course the Jag still had the edge when it came to spontaneously bursting into flames . . . .

Camaro in Decline

Chevrolet General Manager John DeLorean had confidently predicted that Chevrolet would sell more than 200,000 Camaros, but the division produced just 124,901 cars for the 1970 model year, in part because of the shortened model year, but other factors also played a role.

Performance-car sales in general deteriorated in 1970, in large part because the insurance industry had been cracking down on young male drivers. The equation of high-horsepower, low-weight cars plus hormonally addled young drivers yielded the sum of exorbitantly high insurance premiums. While many baby boomers could afford the relatively low prices Chevrolet charged for its Camaros, they were starting to have problems affording the steep costs of insuring the cars.

When the new body style Camaro Z28 debuted in 1970, it was evident that the designers had taken the long hood/short deck formula to new heights. Twin stripes were a Z28 hallmark since 1967, and this continued as the 1970s started.

In the era before insurance companies dictated auto design, stylists could pen beautiful, flowing lines, as seen on the front of the 1970 Z28. The bumper was little better than a token; it was more a stylistic element than proper protection.

Another factor in decreasing Camaro sales was a decreasing customer base. The baby-boom generation was still in the prime of its youth, but a disturbingly large number of them were taken out of the market by the Vietnam War. Throughout the mid-1960s, the U.S. military had been sending troops to Vietnam in increasing numbers. Over half of the Camaro's customer base consisted of males under the age of 25, according to a customer survey published by *Road Test* magazine in August 1970, and, by 1966, nearly 500,000 such American men were traipsing around in the swampy jungles of Vietnam. More than 58,000 U.S. soldiers perished in the conflict. To replenish troop strength, the U.S. army began to increase the number of young males it conscripted into military service. The bulk of these conscripts were young blue-collar males from the very demographic group that bought Camaros.

Yet another factor in decreasing Camaro sales was the fact that baby boomers were aging. The customers that had been in their teens and early twenties when the pony car market exploded were by now in their late twenties and early thirties. More often than not, they had families of their own to support. The snug confines of the Camaro's cabin had been a perfect place for a guy and his girlfriend to spend time in the previous decade. Now this same couple needed something with a bit more space for hauling the kids to little-league practice.

For the first time in Camaro history, side impact beams were built into the huge doors. The second-generation Camaro continued the tradition of offering painful rear seating.

Smog Motors

Judging by outward appearances, Chevrolet sold the same Camaros in 1971 as it had in 1970, and in fact there was quite a bit of confusion regarding model years during this

Over-the-shoulder visibility was compromised by the large B-pillar that the steeply raked rear window required, but few debated that it was a great design. The new design was 2 inches longer and 1.1 inches lower than the 1969 model.

period. This is understandable, since Chevy dealers sold new 1969 models right into February of 1970, then often referred to the 1970 cars as early-release 1971 models, or 1970 1/2 models. The two model years did look almost identical. The most obvious outward change was the use of new bucket seats with higher seatbacks in the 1971 Camaros.

More consequential changes took place underneath the hood for 1971. The year 1970 went down as the peak year for muscle car performance. Beginning in 1971, U.S. automakers began to detune their engines by lowering compression ratios, retarding ignition, installing milder camshafts, and using increasingly restrictive intake and exhaust systems in an attempt to meet toughening pollution-control standards. Horsepower ratings began to drop and would continue to decrease for a generation. To cope with the upcoming removal of lead additives from gasoline—lead would be

incompatible with emissions-control equipment that the government mandated automakers install beginning in 1975—Chevrolet lowered the compression ratio on all the Camaro's optional engines to 8.5:1, with the exception of the LT-1, which was lowered to 9.0:1.

Part of the decrease in the horsepower ratings manufacturers applied to their engines involved the way in which horsepower output was measured. Prior to 1972, most American automakers rated their engines in terms of Society of Automotive Engineers (SAE) gross horsepower, which was measured using a blueprinted test engine running on a stand without accessories, mufflers, or emissions-control devices. This did not provide an accurate measurement of the power output of an installed engine in a street car. Gross horsepower figures were also easily manipulated by carmakers. They could be inflated to make a car appear more muscular or deflated to appease corporate and insurance safetycrats or to qualify a car for a certain class of racing. Beginning in 1971, manufacturers rated engines using the SAE net methods, which measured the power of the engine with all accessories and standard intake and exhaust systems installed. This provided a more accurate measurement of a given car's potential but led to lower overall numbers.

Two rear spoilers were used in 1970: the small unit seen here (RPO D80) and a taller three-piece component (COPO style 9796).

Predictably, the sales of performance cars like the Camaro suffered dramatically. In its May 1971 issue, *Car and Driver* reported:

> . . . the sporty car market itself is withering like last week's roses—it's not nearly as important as it used to be. In 1967, the best year for sporty cars, they captured 11.9 percent of the total car market. Since then, it's been all downhill to the point where 7.2 percent of 1970 auto sales were sporty cars.

Horsepower ratings were down for all engines, thanks to the decreased compression ratios and other changes. Chevrolet listed both SAE gross and SAE net figures for 1971, rating the LT-1 engine in the Z28 at 330 gross horsepower but only 275 net horsepower. It listed the 250 six at 145 gross and 110 net, the 307 at 200 gross and 140 net, the two-barrel 350 at 245 gross and 165 net, the L48 four-barrel 350 in the SS350 at 270 gross and 210 net, and the new LS3 402 in the 396SS at 300 gross and 260 net.

Chevrolet designers used the materials at hand when creating this pre-production 1974 Camaro. Note the lack of emblems, tape on the bumper, and the incorrect wheel covers. *General Motors Corp. Used with permission, GM Media Archives*

The drop in compression ratios marked the end of the L34 and L78 engines in the Camaro SS396. Chevrolet offered no solid-lifter version of the big-block V-8 to replace the L78, and the LS3 replaced the L34. Compression went from the L34's 10.25:1 to 8.5:1, and Chevy engineers reshaped the combustion chambers in attempt to reduce emissions. The LS3 still cranked out 400 lb-ft of torque, which helped it turn in respectable performance numbers. *Hot Rod* ran a 1971 Camaro SS396 through the quarter-mile traps in 14.82 seconds.

The decrease in performance of the solid-lifter LT-1 engine in the Z28 proved even more drastic than the numbers on the spec sheet indicated should be the case. When *Car and Driver* tested a Z28 for its May 1971 issue, it recorded a best quarter-mile time of 15.1 seconds, down nearly a full second from the 14.2-second time turned in by the car it had tested just one year earlier. Chevrolet press people tried to convince the editors that because of production tolerances, power can vary by as much as 15 horsepower in engines built on the same day, meaning that a slow 360-horsepower LT-1 might have

With lower-compression (and lower-horsepower) smog motors and the added weight of the safety bumpers, the zesty performance of the Camaro was fading. To lure buyers, Chevrolet emphasized luxury in 1974. *General Motors Corp. Used with permission, GM Media Archives*

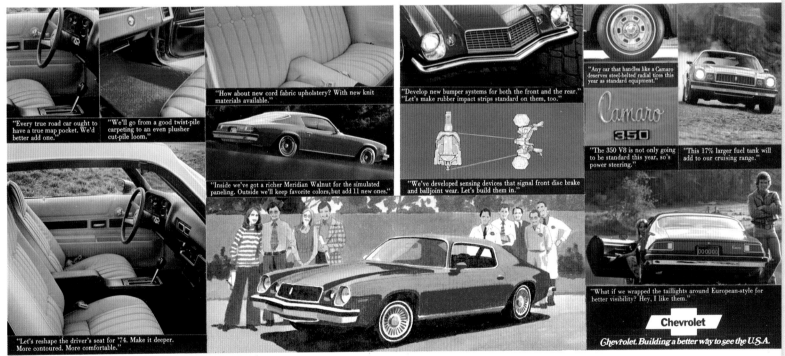

Due to insurance regulations and increasingly strict emissions regulations, Chevrolet started to rely on splashy graphics to catch buyers' eyes. Few Camaros were splashier than the 1974 Z28.

roughly the same power output as a fast 330-horsepower LT-1, but the editors weren't buying it. "There is far more than a 15-horsepower difference between them," the magazine reported.

The decrease in outright performance was bad, but the decrease in normal drivability was worse. Full-throttle performance hadn't been adversely affected nearly as much as part-throttle performance. The Environmental Protection Agency (EPA) conducted its testing at partial-throttle settings, which is how most engines normally operate, so most of the changes to meet emissions involved leaning out the engine at partial-throttle settings. As a result, the early emissions-control engines suffered terribly under normal driving conditions, jerking and bucking and even stalling out under partial-throttle accelerations. A Chevy engineer told *Car and Driver* editors, "All of our engines will respond to more spark [advanced ignition timing] and more fuel because we've got them leaned out so far for emissions." But this was an easier task for the engineers who had developed the complex systems than most backyard

Standard under the long hood of the 1974 Z28 was the L82 350-cubic-inch V-8, rated at 245 horsepower. Aluminum valve covers and intake manifold were part of the package, before engines disappeared beneath hoses and plastic covers.

mechanics, who often took one look at the maze of vacuum hoses under the hood and bought a used car instead.

For the 1971 model year, Chevrolet sold 114,643 Camaros, 4,863 of which were Z28s. The division probably would have sold more cars had it not been for a United Auto Workers union strike that shut down production for 10 weeks right in the prime time for building new 1971 models, from September 15, 1970, until November 20 of that year. Also, the increasingly popular personal luxury cars such as the Cheverolet Monte Carlo were cannibalizing pony-car sales.

As with almost all American vehicles in 1975, flashy paint and vibrant graphics replaced the brute power of prior years. It might not have been fast, but the Camaro Rally Sport was one of the flashiest cars on the road. *General Motors Corp. Used with permission, GM Media Archives*

Vince Piggins' Hail Mary Pass

Vince Piggins hated to see his Z28 devolve into just another Rally Sport-type styling package and suggested developing a version of Chevrolet's 454-cubic-inch LS7 big-block for the Camaro. The engine would be designed for maximum torque, with reshaped cylinder heads, an aluminum high-rise intake, a big Holley carburetor, and a modified camshaft. He failed to get any traction with this idea but convinced management to let him apply these tricks to a version of the 400-cubic-inch small-block used in larger Chevrolet sedans and light trucks.

Piggins produced an engine that sacrificed peak high-rpm horsepower for strong midrange torque. This engine allowed the Z28 to retain its tire-smoking acceleration on the street while still meeting emissions. Piggins proposed making the engine available as an option during the 1971 model year and making it the standard engine in the

Z28 for 1972. He suggested rating the engine at 295 net horsepower, keeping it under the 300-horsepower mark that many insurance companies used as the breaking point for applying high-risk premiums.

Because of decreased sales of all its cars, caused in large part by the 1970 UAW strike, Chevrolet couldn't afford to develop a new engine for a small-volume car like the Camaro, and management worried that without proper development, the engine would be troublesome and unreliable.

Piggins turned to Don Yenko for help. Yenko, the most prolific exploiter of the COPO program, wanted to order 250 Camaros equipped with 400-cubic-inch small-blocks. Piggins suggested to DeLorean that Chevrolet install the version he was developing in the Yenko cars for Beta (customer) testing; if the cars held up for Don Yenko's hard-driving customers, they would be durable enough for anyone.

The two-tone paint on the 1975 Camaro Rally Sport tended to emphasize the long, low stance of the Chevrolet F-body. Body-color wheels were a low-cost method of making the rolling stock stand out. *General Motors Corp. Used with permission, GM Media Archives*

Not every Camaro built in 1977 was a V-8-powered road warrior. The standard Type LT was equipped with a 250-cubic-inch inline six-cylinder engine delivering 110 horsepower (90 in California). It allowed buyers to look good without breaking the bank.

Designing automobiles that gracefully incorporated 5-mile-per-hour bumpers was still a challenge. Compared to some of its contemporaries, the 1977 Camaro Type LT was a clean solution.

Piggins got as far as installing his prototype engine in a test car. Chief Engineer Don McPherson and Chief Camaro Engineer Bob Dorn tested the prototype and came away impressed, but in the face of a rapidly declining pony car market, Chevrolet chose to pass on the 400-cubic-inch Z28.

Bad Goes to Worse

In 1972, its last year of production, the solid-lifter LT-1 generated just 255 net horsepower in the Camaro, reflecting Chevrolet engineers' struggle to maintain performance levels in the face of increasingly stringent emissions regulations. The original Z28 had been a tire-smoking monster; the 1972 Z28 could barely chirp the tires.

The big-block V-8 made its last appearance in the Camaro for the 1972 model year. That year, the LS3 generated just 240 horsepower (net) and 345 lb-ft of torque. Very few people seemed interested in a 240-horsepower big-block or high-performance cars in general. Chevrolet sold just 6,562 Camaro SS models and only 2,575 Z28s. In all, the division sold 68,651 total Camaros, making 1972 the worst year yet for Camaro sales.

The low numbers for 1972 again reflect the results of a disastrous UAW strike at the Norwood, Ohio, assembly plant where General Motors built its F-body cars, but the main problem seemed to be that buyers weren't interested in castrated Camaros,

which is a bit of a shame, since in some ways the cars were actually getting better. The power ratings may have been plummeting, but Chevrolet engineers were starting to come to grips with emissions-control equipment and had begun to solve some of the lean-carburetion problems, leading to cars that were smoother running, though still not as smooth as pre-smog-motor cars.

At least the cars with hydraulic lifters were smoother running; it was becoming increasingly clear that there was no place for a solid-lifter LT-1 in Chevrolet's new, emissions-friendly lineup, and 1972 proved to be its final year. For 1973, the Z28 engine received hydraulic lifters, along with a corresponding decrease in horsepower, from 255 net in 1972 to 245 net in 1973.

Horsepower levels fell even more precipitously for the other engines in the 1973 lineup. The 250 six sunk to 100 horsepower, and the 307 V-8 generated just 15 more

Camaro Type LT buyers tended to be a bit more mainstream, eschewing flashy graphics. For 1977, Chevrolet curried favor with these buyers by offering tasteful striping, cross-lace alloy wheels, and white-wall tires. The suspension leaned toward comfort rather than performance.

As the car-buying public's taste shifted towards personal luxury cars like the Monte Carlo, pony car interiors moved increasingly upscale throughout the 1970s.

than that. The two-barrel 350 netted just 145 horsepower, and the four-barrel L48 version of that engine generated a measly 175 horsepower.

A Near-Death Experience

In some ways, the worst fears of GM management had come to fruition by 1973. Model proliferation proved to be as problematic as Bunkie Knudsen had feared when he decided not to approve the mini Riviera designed by Bill Mitchell and Irv Rybicki. In 1963, Chevrolet produced three basic automobile platforms: the Corvair, the Chevy II, and the full-sized sedans. The various permutations of these vehicles, such as Monza, Nova SS, Bel Air, and Impala SS, amounted to glorified trim packages. This kept production processes simple and inexpensive. But by 1973, model proliferation had created a bewildering line-up that was complicated and expensive to produce. It was also a nightmare to market, and led to a situation where similar models were cannibalizing sales from each other without increasing Chevrolet Division's overall share of the auto market.

When GM management started counting the beans needed to develop safety and emissions equipment for Chevrolet's Byzantine product line, and then certifying each of these vehicles with all the various state and federal agencies involved, it became crystal clear that the division would need to simplify its product offering. A slow-selling car like the Camaro appeared an obvious candidate for elimination.

Upcoming bumper regulations that would require a redesign of the Camaro's front subframe provided GM President Ed Cole the excuse he needed to announce the end of Camaro and Firebird production, but a core group of enthusiasts within the corporation lobbied for a stay of execution. In addition, dealer support helped save the Camaro. A group of dealers traveled to Motor City and personally committed to selling the entire Camaro production run if GM kept the car in Chevrolet's lineup. In *Camaro*, Gary Witzenburg quotes Bob Dorn, the chief engineer for the Camaro at that time:

> . . . the bumper standards were coming upon us for '73, and it looked like we would have to spend a fair amount of money to put a new front end on [the Camaro]. So we said, well, we won't do a new front end . . . we'll gin it up with struts and whatever we have to do.

The large, three-piece spoiler was popular on the 1977 Camaro Type LT. This option, RPO D80, included a front and rear spoiler and cost $87. Occasionally, the factory had difficulty lining up the rear spoiler end caps with the center section.

Chevrolet mounted a slew of high-performance parts in its 1977 Camaro Z28 to create the canyon-carver available in showrooms. Note the drum brakes on the rear axle. *General Motors Corp. Used with permission, GM Media Archives*

The convertible had disappeared from the Camaro lineup in 1970, but buyers wanting fresh air and blue sky could soon order the optional T-top roof.

Development focused as much on keeping tooling costs low as it did on meeting federal impact standards. Chevrolet's engineers succeeded on both fronts, and in what amounts to a minor regulatory miracle, they "ginned up" the front end with enough struts and reinforcements to save even the pretty RS nose design, though according to Dorn, under the skin it "looked like a NASCAR stock car, it had so many rods and struts behind those little bumpers."

The engineers' hard work not only saved the RS nose piece, it saved the Camaro itself, since GM management could not use the cost of redesigning the front end as an excuse to axe Chevrolet's most sophisticated and advanced automobile platform at that time.

The Camaro Type LT made its last appearance in 1978, replaced in 1979 by the Berlinetta. This example features an aftermarket T-roof.

Most 1978 Camaro Type LTs were equipped with automatic transmissions. The four-speed manual was something of a rarity in a vehicle designed for effortless cruising.

Type LT

The struts, braces, and rods added weight to the Camaro, but only by 16 pounds over the previous year. The Camaro had been saved, though the Super Sport package expired along with the last big-block Camaro engine in 1972. In its place, Chevrolet offered the new Type LT Coupe for 1973. In keeping with Detroit's general trend of trading performance for comfort and convenience, the "LT" in "Type LT" stood for "Luxury Touring."

The Type LT featured many of the same standard-equipment pieces as the previous Super Sport, including special identification badges, tachometer, temperature gauge, ammeter, clock, and 7-inch styled wheels with chrome trim rings, but it also featured a host of luxury accessories, such as tilt steering wheel, deluxe seat trim, wood-grained

Above: In an effort to hold down costs, Chevrolet equipped the 1979 Camaro Z28 with stamped-steel wheels. However, they were painted body color to inject visual pizzazz.

Opposite: In 1979, Chevrolet sold more Z28s than in any previous year of prodcution—84,879.

Chevrolet introduced a wraparound front chin spoiler on the 1979 Z28 in an effort to improve aerodynamics and fuel efficiency. The louvers on the front fenders were functional, venting hot air from the engine compartment.

finish on the doors and instrument panels, lighted glove box, right- and left-hand sport mirrors, and sport steering wheel.

Unlike the RS trim package, the Type LT had its own base engine, the L65, a 350-cubic-inch V-8 with a four-barrel carburetor that generated 165 horsepower, though a buyer could select the optional 175-horsepower L48, provided he or she didn't live in California, since the L48 didn't meet that state's strict emissions standards. Unlike the Super Sports it replaced, the Type LT could be ordered in conjunction with the RS trim package and the Z28, so it was possible to get a Type LT Z28 RS. This combination could even be ordered with air conditioning, since the elimination of solid lifters in the LT-1 engine allowed air conditioning to be offered as an option on the Z28 for the first time in the model's history.

Pontiac Keeps the Faith

In just four model years, the Camaro had devolved from a balls-out high-performance muscle car to a tepid luxury coupe. The Camaro wasn't the only car to suffer. By 1973, it seemed that the muscle car era was dead and gone. Even Chrysler's mighty Hemi had disappeared.

But Pontiac wasn't about to roll over in submission just yet. In 1973, when every other manufacturer had abandoned performance, Pontiac built the Super Duty 455, an engine option available on the Formula and Trans Am versions of the division's F-body Firebird.

The SD455 engine combined every high-performance piece remaining in Pontiac's parts catalog—radical camshaft, big carburetor, four-bolt main-bearing caps, forged connecting rods, aluminum flat-top pistons—in a last-ditch effort to keep emissions

As in prior years, the 1979 Camaro Z28 enjoyed a full slate of performance enhancements, including a close-ratio four-speed transmission, dual exhaust, special springs and shock absorbers, and a 350-cubic-inch V-8 rated at 175 horsepower (170 in the Golden State).

Not for the shy, the 1979 Camaro Z28 used a blacked-out treatment on the grille, headlight, and parking light bezels, and a large decal surrounding the nonfunctional hood scoop.

regulations from throttling the fun out of performance cars. With a low 8.4:1 compression ratio, the engine was rated at 290 net horsepower and 390 lb-ft of torque, but those ratings were unrealistically low for insurance reasons, as the cars' 13-second quarter-mile ETs testified.

Pontiac got a late start building SD455 Firebirds and only produced 396 examples in 1973. In 1974, Pontiac built 943 SD455 Formulas and Trans Ams before the engine fell victim to rising gas prices and increasing emissions controls.

Power Decreases and Sales Increase

The Camaro might have been in the midst of a precipitous fall in horsepower output, and it might have played second fiddle to the Super Duty versions of the rival F-body cars from Pontiac, but Camaro production increased by nearly 50 percent in 1973, to 96,752 cars. Better yet, Z28 production rose over four-fold, to 11,575 units. Super Duty Firebirds might have out-muscled the Z28 by 45 horsepower (at least on paper; the difference as measured at the rear wheels would have been much greater), but to do that the Pontiacs required a nearly 30 percent increase in cubic-inch displacement.

The 1973 oil crisis that began on October 17, 1973, when Arab members of the Organization of Petroleum Exporting Countries (OPEC) announced that they would no longer ship petroleum to the United States and its allies in Western Europe, was a major factor in the buying public's abandonment of big-block engines, Super Duty or otherwise. The effects of the embargo were immediate, and the price of oil quadrupled by 1974. The embargo ended on March 17, 1974, but it had the lasting effect of

In 1979, the Camaro had its best sales year ever, with Chevrolet selling 282,582 units.

Chevrolet's engineers and stylists worked together to reduce aerodynamic drag, and the 1979 Camaro Z28 grille opening had gotten smaller to reduce drag. More of the engine-cooling air then came from openings underneath the front bumper.

In a vehicle like the 1979 Camaro Z28, it was necessary to have large doors to allow access to the rear seats. The sheer size of the doors could pose a challenge in a tight parking lot or on a grade.

encouraging car buyers, even buyers shopping for performance cars, to gravitate toward small-block V-8s like the 350-cubic-inch powerplant found in the Z28 instead of big-block V-8s like Pontiac's SD455.

The dwindling supply of used performance cars proved another factor contributing to increased Z28 sales. When the smog-motored 1971 cars hit the market, high-compression muscle cars from previous years were plentiful and cheap on the used-car market, but

these cars were driven hard, more often than not competing in races both legal and illegal, and by 1973, attrition had begun to take a serious toll on their numbers. Plus, it was becoming increasingly difficult and expensive to find the high-octane fuel required to keep the previous generation of performance cars on the road. As the new generation became more drivable—if less powerful—its appeal to performance-car buyers began to grow.

Tape graphics on the lower portion of the door identified the 1979 Camaro Z28 to all. Finned turbine-look wheels were attractive but a pain in the butt to clean.

Camaro at a Crossroads

The Camaro survived its near-death experience for the 1973 model year and even posted a healthy sales increase, but that didn't guarantee the car's survival. Sales may have increased, but they still languished below the 100,000 mark.

Ford's planned changes for the 1974 Mustang meant even more uncertainty for the Camaro's future. Ford planned to take its pony car in a radically new direction, basing the next-generation Mustang on its popular Pinto subcompact platform. Today, we know that the Pinto was one of the all-time worst cars in automotive history, and that the 1974–1978 Mustang II, which was basically a stretched version of the Pinto, was only incrementally better than its turd-like Pinto progenitor. But at the time, Ford was selling every Pinto it could build and the move seemed logical. In fact it was, from a business perspective; Ford sold an astonishing 385,993 Mustang IIs for the 1974 model year, proving that the combination of Watergate, our humiliating defeat in Vietnam, and the Arab oil embargo had effectively caused the United States' buying public to lose its collective mind.

The automotive press buzzed with rumors that Chevrolet would follow suit and build its next-generation Camaro from the Vega platform. The Vega, Chevrolet's subcompact Pinto competitor, was arguably a better car than the Pinto if for no other reason than it lacked the Pinto's propensity to burst into flames when hit from behind, but that advantage pretty much filled the entire list of good things to say about the Vega.

Fortunately, the rumored car was not a Camaro replacement. The "spectacular 2+2 roadster," as described by John DeLorean in the *Detroit News,* was the Monza, a Vega-based coupe introduced for the 1975 model year. Like the Vega, the only notable virtue of the Monza was that it was less likely to burst into flames than a Pinto. To be fair, the Monza could have been a ground breaking car if it had received its intended engine—a high-output Wankel rotary unit. Development problems regarding engine seals and excessive fuel comsumption shelved plans for a rotary engine at the last minute, leaving engineers scrambling to install piston-driven powerplants.

The Camaro soldiered on for 1974 with what amounted to a facelift. The car received proper safety bumpers front and rear, replacing the "ginned up" system used in 1973 and killing the twin-bumper Rally Sport front end once and for all. In fact, the Rally Sport package disappeared for 1974, but Chevrolet kept the 245-horsepower Z28 in the lineup, the main changes to the model consisting of bold new graphics and aluminum trim pieces along the rocker panels. The availability of optional radial tires pushed the already-excellent handling of the Z28 to new levels, helping the model earn *Car* magazine's "Performance Car of the Year" award.

As the 1970s drew to a close, the 1979 Camaro Z28 showed how interior design was leaning to a monochromatic look. Well-bolstered seats held occupants in place during spirited maneuvers.

Chevrolet ensured that drivers in the wake of the 1979 Camaro Z28 knew what they were following with the use of a full-width tape stripe beneath the rear spoiler. Access to the fuel filler was behind the door in the center of the rear panel.

The Type LT had proven a popular addition to the Camaro lineup, and for 1974, Chevrolet added even more "L" to the Luxury-Touring equation, increasing sound-deadening insulation and adding new fabrics to the interior. The American automobile was entering the age of plush velour interiors, an interior-styling excess that would rival the exterior tailfins of the 1950s for sheer ostentation. "Luxury" was rapidly replacing "performance" as a buzzword in automotive marketing, thanks in large part to adoption of a nationwide 55-mile-per-hour speed limit in 1974—a "temporary" measure that would last well into the next decade.

Engine offerings remained basically the same. The unloved 307 V-8 went the way of the unloved Powerglide automatic transmission, which had made its last appearance on the Camaro's option list in 1972. The base engine for the V-8 coupe became the 145-horsepower two-barrel version of the 350. In a move that bucked automotive trends of the period, the L48 version of the 350 gained rather than lost horsepower, going from 175 horsepower in 1973 to 185 in 1974.

IROC

In 1973, Roger Penske and Riverside International Raceway President Les Richter developed the International Race of Champions (IROC), a racing series that gathered champions from all types of motorsports and pitted them against one another in identically prepared cars. The organizers selected Porsche 911 RSRs for the first running of the series but in 1974 chose Camaro Z28s.

Since the races were televised, this selection gave the Z28—and the Camaro in general—an extremely high profile, helping boost sales by more than 50 percent. Chevrolet built 151,008 Camaros for the 1974 model year, 13,802 of which were Z28s, making 1974 the second-best year yet for the hottest Camaro. This increase came at a time when overall auto sales were down almost across the board.

Looking like it had been dipped in a bucket of blue paint, the 1980 Camaro Z28 used a Z28-only V-8 displacing 350 cubic inches and generating 190 horsepower. However, California Z28 buyers had to deal with a 305-cubic-inch V-8 rated at 155 horsepower.

Never one to let a good design fade prematurely, the 1980 Camaro Z28 utilized the same style of painted stamped-steel wheel that had been used for quite a few years. Strong, cheap, and good looking, it was one of Chevrolet's better ideas.

Catalytic Converters

The worldwide auto industry had been preparing for 1975 since the end of the previous decade. This would be the year in which a host of environmental regulations took effect. The most significant of these would be the installation of catalytic converters on all 1975 model-year cars. These consisted of canisters filled with a catalyst—platinum-coated beads, usually—installed in the exhaust pipes of cars. These catalysts would ignite unburned hydrocarbons in the exhaust gases and achieve a dramatic decrease in carbon monoxide emissions while at the same time allowing engineers to better tune carburetion and improve the drivability problems that plagued early smog motors. This new device required the burning of unleaded gasoline, since lead would clog up

Rear wheel spats were fitted in front of the wheel opening in an effort to direct airflow around the rear tires. Similar aero aids were installed on the Pontiac Trans Am.

the converters and require expensive repairs. This proved to be a positive development as the negative health effects of lead became more widely known. At the time, however, it was viewed in a negative light, since lead had made possible the high-compression, high-horsepower engines of the previous decade.

Rather than reengineer the Z28's 245-horsepower LT-1 engine, with its 9.0:1 compression ratio, to make it work with unleaded, low-octane gasoline, Chevrolet decided to kill the Z28 model. The optional L48 version of the 350 V-8 also expired after 1974, replaced by the LM1 engine, the only optional engine available in a Camaro for 1975. This boat anchor of an engine generated a measly 155 horsepower and 250 lb-ft of torque, marking the all-time low point for the power output of Chevrolet's pony car. *Car and Driver* ran a 1975 LM1-equipped Camaro through the quarter-mile in 16.8 seconds, making it the slowest V-8-powered Camaro ever tested by a car magazine. In

Body-color bumper caps lent a unified visual look to the 1980 Z28. Starting retail price for the Z28 was $7,121.32, and with sales of 45,137 units, it continued to be a strong seller.

The blacked-out grille, headlight, and parking light treatment made the Red Orange finish (paint code 76) even more striking. The color was applied to 4,374 Camaros in 1980.

Opposite: To maintain the handling reputation that the Z28 had earned, the 1980 version used beefy stabilizer bars, P225/70R-15 radials, heavy-duty springs, and 1-inch piston shock absorbers with special valving.

terms of performance, the Camaro had bottomed out; from 1975 on the car had nowhere to go but up, though it would take another 16 years before power would once again equal the 245 horsepower cranked out by the 1974 Z28s.

Killing the Z28 fit in with General Motors' corporate philosophy of downplaying performance and emphasizing luxury and flash. Though the Camaro was once again selected as the 1975 IROC car, GM did not capitalize on this with special editions or increased promotion. Instead, Chevrolet lavished even more luxury on the Type LT Sport Coupe

All Camaros received the most dramatic visual change of 1975: the wrap-around rear window. In addition to improved rearward visibility, this larger window gave the Camaro a more modern, airy appearance. It also gave the car a much less aggressive appearance. Sales were down slightly at 145,775 cars, but not nearly down as much as auto sales in general, and the Camaro's future became a bit more secure.

In 1976, the Camaro returned virtually unchanged. The Type LT got another dose of "L," all cars got a little more safety and emissions equipment, and the LM1 engine got 10 more horsepower and 10 more lb-ft of torque. Sales rose to 182,981. This had the Camaro nipping at the heels of the Mustang, which sold 187,567 units that year, but by this time, the Pinto-based Mustang was no longer in the Camaro's league when it came to performance. (The Mustang II was not even in the same performance league as the original Chevy II of 15 years earlier.)

The functional hood vents were redesigned for 1980, presenting a cleaner appearance. The Z28 was fitted with a rear-facing, solenoid-activated flapper door on the hood that flipped open under full throttle to feed cool air to the carburetor.

A Kick in the Ass from Pontiac

In the middle of the 1977 model year, Chevrolet once again began offering Z28 versions of the Camaro. For that, Camaro fans can probably thank the folks over at Pontiac Division; they'd been keeping the muscle-car concept alive—even if it was on life support—throughout the 1970s. Pontiac used the Trans Am version of its F-body Firebird as the ultimate expression of the division's commitment to high performance.

Trans Am sales started coming on strong in 1974, the last year that Chevrolet produced the Z28. In 1974—the last year Pontiac offered the 290-horsepower Super Duty 455 as an option—the division sold 10,255 Trans Ams to Chevrolet's 13,802 Z28s. For 1975, the highest performing engine in the Trans Am lineup was the L75 version of the 455-cubic-inch engine, which generated just 200 horsepower but still cranked out a respectable 330 lb-ft of torque. This wasn't terribly impressive, but it did trump the paltry 155-horsepower and 250 lb-ft of torque generated by the LM1 in the Camaro. With no high-performance competition from Chevrolet (or from Ford or Chrysler, for that matter), Pontiac sold 27,274 Trans Ams in 1975. Horsepower levels didn't improve for 1976, but sales did; Pontiac sold 46,704 Trans Ams that year.

In 1977, the 455-cubic-inch V-8 went away for good, but the 400-cubic-inch L78T/A engine now generated the same 200 horsepower as the big motor had, with only a 5 lb-ft drop in torque. For 1978, Pontiac engineers coaxed another 20 horsepower from the T/A version of the L78 at the expense of another 5 lb-ft drop in torque output. This made the 220-horsepower 1978 Trans Am, with its 320 lb-ft of torque, the strongest American muscle car sold during the last years of the decade. Sales of the car

showed that performance still mattered to American auto buyers. Pontiac sold 68,745 Trans Ams in 1977 and 93,341 Trans Ams in 1978.

The Trans Am had more going for it than just performance. Pontiac marketers had a much better understanding of the value of promotion than Chevrolet marketers. Hal Needham had given the Trans Am a costarring role in his 1977 hit film *Smokey and the Bandit*; it could be argued that the car turned in the best performance of the film. Where Chevrolet Division had failed to capitalize on the selection of the Camaro for the IROC racing series, Pontiac promoted the hell out of black-and-gold Bandit-replica Trans Ams.

Camaro sales also climbed during this period, rising to a total of 218,854 units in 1977, but Chevrolet had nothing to counter Pontiac's Trans Am. As the continued performance levels of the Trans Am indicated, it was possible to extract acceptable power from an engine with smog controls; Chevrolet had abandoned the Z28 as much because of corporate timidity as it had because of technological challenges. Within a year of dropping the Z28, it was clear that Chevrolet management had made a mistake, and the division resumed emphasizing performance.

A 350-cubic-inch engine developing 190 horses was standard in the 49-state Camaro Z28 for 1980. As engine reliability increased, there were fewer reasons to get under the hood, so engine compartment appearance was a diminishing priority for Chevrolet.

Next page: The 1980 Camaro Z28 rode on the same 108-inch wheelbase as the original 1967 Camaro. However, the newer Camaro was 13 inches longer, 2 inches wider, and almost 2 inches lower.

Under heavy cornering, a 1980 Z28 equipped with T-tops suffered a bit of cowl shake when compared to a non-T-top equipped vehicle, but the vast majority of driving was at speeds less than 10/10ths. This popular option allowed fresh air and sunlight into the cabin, yet the vehicle could be locked up more securely than a traditional convertible.

The easiest and least expensive way to resurrect the Camaro's performance image was to capitalize on the IROC connection, since that required no engineering or development costs. Chevrolet soon began running Camaro ads featuring images of IROC cars and racers. More importantly, the division began planning to resurrect the Z28.

A New Z28

The Camaro development team did not want the new Z28 to be another trim package, like the Rally Sport or Type LT, but no one was quite sure what they did want the car to be. In the age of smog-strangled low-compression engines, no one quite knew what a high-performance car was anymore. Chief Camaro Engineer Tom Zimmer had development engineer Jack Turner begin working on turning the Z28 chassis into a

Trans Am beater, a tall order, given that the Trans Am had developed a reputation as a superb-handling sport coupe.

For the car to stand out, it would need something more than the optional Z41 performance suspension package. Turner and his crew developed a suspension system that consisted of specially tuned front and rear stabilizer bars, revalved shocks, recalibrated spring rates, and different bushings, grommets, and attachment hardware all designed to complement the GR70-15 steel-belted radial tires that came as standard equipment on the Z28. Pontiac had long been tuning its suspensions to take advantage of radial-tire technology, and now Chevrolet would follow suit.

Engineers would bump the power output of the LM1 engine to a relatively healthy 170 horsepower and 270 lb-ft of torque, the same rating that the engine had in other versions of the Camaro, but when mounted in the Z28, which featured a less-restrictive exhaust system, the actual output was a bit higher. Chevrolet kept the advertised ratings the same to avoid alerting the EPA to the exhaust-system changes, which would require the division to go through the trouble and expense of certifying the Z28 V-8 as a separate engine. The result was a car that, while rated at 30 horsepower less than the Trans Am on paper, would hold its own against the Pontiac on the street. Both *Hot Rod* and *Motor Trend* magazines recorded 15.4-second quarter-mile times, besting the 16.9 seconds generated by *Car and Driver* in a 6.6-liter (400-cubic-inch) Trans Am, though once again this in part reflects the aggressive technique used by the testers at *Hot Rod*, who were notorious for clutchless speed shifts. In the real world, the 1977 Z28 and Trans Am were roughly equal in outright acceleration.

While Chevrolet's development team didn't want to make the Z28 just another trim package, it did want to make the car stand out from the Camaro crowd, so the Z28 got a full complement of badges, stripes, and special paint. The most obvious change was the addition of the fake NACA-duct hood scoop, or rather, a NACA-duct hood-scoop decal; instead of a fake hood scoop, the 1977 1/2 Z28 had a *fake* fake hood scoop, which somehow seems an appropriate metaphor for the era.

Even with its sleeper engine, the Z28's excellent handling proved to be its most outstanding feature. Fans appreciated the new Z28 and, when final production numbers came in, Chevrolet had sold 14,347 Z28s. Customers and dealers clamored for the Z28, but conservative forcasts led Chevrolet product planners to order too few components to build more cars. Though still well off from the number of Trans Ams Pontiac built, this represented a successful year for the Z28, especially considering that the model was only on sale for half a year. The 218,853 Camaros sold in 1977 marked another milestone for Chevrolet's pony car—for the first time ever, the Camaro outsold Ford's Mustang.

More Power, More Sales

Chevrolet kept changes to a minimum for the next four years; most of its resources were going toward developing the third-generation Camaro, to be introduced for the 1982 model year. Designers restyled the front and rear bumpers once again to better

When *Car and Driver* magazine put the whip to a 1980 Z28 in its April 1980 issue, the tester turned in a quarter-mile performance of 16.4 seconds at 86 miles per hour in a car equipped with a four-speed and 3.08:1 rear axle ratio. Sixty miles per hour came up in 8.5 seconds, while top speed was 120 miles per hour.

integrate the hardware and the body, leading to smoother, cleaner lines. In 1979, Chevrolet replaced the "Type LT" name with "Berlinetta," following the then-current trend of giving luxury coupes names either taken from or sounding like they were taken from the Romantic languages.

Engine options changed little during the period, with horsepower ratings going up or down by small increments each year. The base 250 six rose to 115 horsepower in 1979 but fell back down to 110 in 1981. A 305-cubic-inch V-8 that had replaced the two-barrel version of the 350 in 1976 rose from 140 horsepower in 1976 to 165 horsepower in 1981. The top-of-the-line LM1 350 in the Z28 went from 170 horsepower in 1977 to 185 horsepower in 1978, then fell to 175 horsepower in 1979.

In 1980, LM1 power output rose to a best-ever 190 horsepower and 280 lb-ft of torque, thanks in part to a functional fresh-air induction system. In 1978, Chevrolet designers replaced the hood-scoop-like decal with an honest-to-goodness fake hood scoop. This matched the fender vents designers added that year. To argue whether the fake hood scoop was an improvement over the *fake* fake hood scoop would probably be putting too fine a point on the issue. Few would argue that the 1980 addition of a *real* hood scoop—that actually funneled cold air into the carburetor, helping to achieve an increase of 15 horsepower—was anything but good. But like all good things, the bump in power came to an end; in 1981, the last year of the second-generation Camaro's product life cycle, power fell back to 175 horsepower.

Sales were up again for 1978, with Chevrolet selling a record 272,633 Camaros, 54,907 of which were Z28s. Sales rose again in 1979, with yet another record number of Camaros sold: 282,582 units. The truly amazing sales number of that year was the 84,879 Z28 versions of the Camaro that Chevrolet sold. While fewer than the 117,109 Trans Ams Pontiac sold in 1979, it still represented a major achievement for the division—in one year, Chevrolet had sold more Z28 models than it had sold combined during the Camaro's first 11 years of production.

Chevrolet could be proud of the performance of the Camaro both on the road and in the showrooms, but everyone at the division knew that the GM F-bodies' domination of the performance-car market would soon end. The cars that had seemed so fresh and modern in 1970 looked bloated and antiquated in 1980.

Plus, the cars faced new competition from Ford, which had abandoned the Pinto-based shit-box Mustang II for 1979 and introduced a completely new car using the most modern chassis architecture in Ford's product line. The new Ford pony car presented a serious challenge. Even though Chevrolet sold a record number of Camaros in 1979, the Mustang outsold it, with Ford moving 369,936 examples of its revitalized pony car.

Camaro sales fell to 152,021 units in 1980; in 1981, sales fell further still, to 126,139 units. By the 1982 model year, it was time for a new pony car from Chevrolet.

CHAPTER FOUR

THE BEST-HANDLING CAR IN AMERICA

In 1982, a Camaro once again paced the Indianapolis 500, this time to commemorate the introduction of the newest Camaro. The Z28 that was used on the track needed no modifications to handle pace car chores.

A principled gearhead could have been forgiven for having suicidal thoughts as the dismal 1970s gave way to the 1980s, which looked to be an even bleaker decade for automotive enthusiasts. Horsepower levels for GM's F-body cars were sinking almost as fast as the economic indicators of the time.

Pontiac had abandoned its high-performance, big-cube engines after a small run of Trans Ams fitted with the division's 6.6-liter, 220-horsepower L-78 engine in 1979. In 1980, the division boosted its 301-cubic-inch V-8 with a primitive draw-through, carbureted turbocharging system. The blown engine produced 210 horsepower and 345 lb-ft of torque—impressive numbers for the period, at least on paper; in reality, the turbo lag inherent in the design meant a driver almost had enough time to pop in the latest Greg Kihn Band cassette tape between the moment he stepped on the accelerator and when the little engine came to a boil. In 1981, output fell to 200 horsepower and 340 lb-ft of torque.

Above: It's traditional for Indianapolis pace car replicas to be festooned with graphics that highlight that model's role in the 500-mile race. The 1982 Z28 Camaro Indy pace car was no exception, with the race logo affixed to the B-pillar.

Left: The standard engine in the 1982 Camaro Indianapolis 500 pace car replica was the carbureted LG4 5.0-liter V-8, rated at 145 horsepower. The only optional engine was the fuel-injected LU5 5.0-liter V-8, cranking out 165 horsepower.

The NACA ducts on the hood were nonfunctional, but they were a significant styling feature. Model years 1982 and 1983 Z28s used fiberglass hoods; steel stampings entered production in 1984.

In a sorry comment on the state of the performance car of that period, the 200-horsepower Turbo Trans Am was the most powerful U.S.-built performance car in 1981. The Corvette had sunk to 190 horsepower, and the Z28 generated just 175 horsepower from its 350-cubic-inch LM1 V-8. Ford's Mustang was in even sorrier shape. The largest engine in the Mustang—a 255-cubic-inch boat anchor that was essentially a 302-cubic-inch V-8 with the bore reduced—produced a paltry 118 horsepower. American performance cars had bottomed out.

The one positive aspect of hitting bottom is that there is nowhere to go but up, and in 1982 the situation did begin to improve. General Motors deserves the lion's share of credit for this improvement, because in 1982, GM introduced completely new F-body cars.

It was time for a new Camaro. When the second-generation car had been introduced in 1970, the president of General Motors at that time, Pete Estes, had predicted the car was such an advanced design that it would remain in the lineup for 12 years. The car had indeed held on for 12 years, most of those being successful, but sales had fallen over 50 percent between the peak year of 1979 and 1981, the last year of the second-generation design.

Front-Wheel-Drive Camaros

Chevrolet began development work on the third-generation Camaro in 1975. That year, two design teams—one overseen by Jerry Palmer and another directed by Bill Porter—began developing the third-generation Camaro, which was originally planned as a 1980 model-year car.

Chevrolet sold 6,360 1982 Indianapolis 500 pace car replicas, RPO option Z50 ($10,600). All pace car replicas were built in Chevrolet's Van Nuys, California, plant between mid-March and late April.

There were a number of differences between the actual 1982 Indy 500 pace cars and the street-legal replicas, most notable among them being that the track cars had 250-horsepower alumium-block engines, a light bar, an ABC TV camera in the rear, and a 140-mile-per-hour speedometer.

In 1975, the entire auto industry was moving toward front-wheel-drive cars, and almost every passenger car General Motors was developing used a front-wheel-drive configuration. As it had done with the Corvair, Chevrolet turned to Germany for inspiration, evaluating a Volkswagen Scirocco front-wheel-drive sport coupe as a benchmark for the new Camaro.

At the time, Chevrolet engineers were developing the division's first front-wheel-drive car—the Citation—and considered using components from that car for the next-generation Camaro. Once again, a core group of enthusiasts within General Motors saved the corporation's F-body pony cars. These folks pointed out that the Citation's front-wheel-drive architecture wasn't strong enough to handle a V-8 engine, which everyone agreed was a prerequisite for a successful pony car.

Basing the third-generation Camaro on the lowly Citation would have made impossible the primary directive of the upcoming Chevy pony car's chassis engineers: make the new Z28 out-handle the Trans Am. The previous Z28 had handled very well, but it hadn't wrested the best-handling-American-car title away from Pontiac. When equipped with the optional WS-6 handling package that by then included four-wheel power disc brakes, the Trans Am out-handled even Chevrolet's Corvette sports car.

The question whether or not to go with a front-wheel-drive design still hadn't been resolved when Bill Mitchell retired in July 1977. In fact, Pontiac designers were still lobbying to make the F-bodies front-wheel-drive as late as 1979, though concept approval of what would become the final F-body designs had already been given in February 1978. All of this uncertainty and change hindered development of the third-generation Camaro. By the time Irv Rybicki took over as head of design in August 1977, the decision had been made to move production out to 1982, fulfilling Estes' prophecy of the Camaro having a dozen-year lifespan.

Renderings of the 1982 Camaro circulated around Chevrolet's design studios in 1978 and 1979 as stylists sought the ideal mix of aggressiveness, stance, and affordability. The 1982 Berlinetta series was finalized by the fall of 1980. *General Motors Corp. Used with permission, GM Media Archives*

It seems everyone wanted a Z28 in 1984, what with 52,457 being built with the RPO L69 5.0-liter V-8. This engine was rated at 190 horsepower and breathed through a four-barrel Rochester Quadrajet carburetor.

More and more, automobiles were ingesting cooling air for the engine from underneath the nose, as seen on the 1984 Z28. The flexible air dam beneath the long overhang helped to direct air up toward the radiator.

Building a World-Beating Camaro

Even though the second-generation Camaro had overstayed its welcome, it still provided a tough act to follow. Because powertrain engineers had just begun developing technologies like fuel-injection systems that would enable them to produce acceptable levels of horsepower and meet emissions requirements, the Camaro's design team knew there would not be huge gains in engine power output; hence performance gains would need to come from an improved power-to-weight ratio. The 1981 Z28 had weighed 3,660 pounds. The fourth-generation car would have to be smaller and lighter if it was to be faster and handle better than its predecessor.

The second-generation Camaro had evolved into a huge, baroque car festooned with scoops, spoilers, and vents. The third-generation car would return to a clean, simple

design devoid of overwrought graphics and bolted-on appendages. Even on the sporty Z28 version of the car, all striping and badges would be below the bumper line, moving away from the psychedelic graphics splashed across the flanks of the previous Z28.

The most striking aspect of the new car would be its large hatchback window, a complex piece of glass with compound curves that proved a serious challenge to manufacture. It was, in fact, the largest piece of automotive glass ever produced up until that time.

The hermaphroditic system of unit-body and front subframe used since the original Chevy II would be abandoned once and for all in the new F-bodies; instead, they would have a fully unitized chassis. This allowed designers to use a more modern MacPherson strut front suspension design, though chassis engineers chose to retain the traditional worm-and-roller steering system for the base cars and a recirculating-ball system for

Performance was starting a strong resurgence, as evidenced by the 190 horsepower under the long hood of the 1984 Z28. Engine-displacement badging was subtly mounted on the forward end of the rocker panel.

Chevrolet's engineers mounted the third-generation Z28's engine as far back as possible in an effort to improve the vehicle's performance by moving the vehicle's center of gravity close to the center of the car. Servicing the engine could prove a challenge.

the Z28. These designs had long been abandoned by the manufacturers of European sport coupes in favor of rack-and-pinion systems, which impart a much more direct feel to the steering wheel.

The third-generation car's retention of the live-axle rear suspension also diverged from the accepted practices of European designers. Chevrolet's design team considered an independent rear suspension instead of the Camaro's traditional solid-axle (also referred to as "live axle") design but abandoned the idea as too time-consuming to design and too expensive to build. They did come up with an innovative take on the traditional live axle, however. They abandoned the leaf springs previously used on the Camaro and adopted a design that used stamped sheetmetal lower control arms, lateral track bars, fore-aft torque arms, and coil springs to locate the axle and control its motions.

For $179, buyers of the new Camaro could purchase four-wheel disc brakes—RPO J65—for the first time since 1969, putting the Camaro at least on par with Pontiac's WS-6-equipped Trans Am.

While developing a modern unit-body frame for the new Camaro ate up valuable development time, it helped contribute to the 1982 Camaro's 3,300-pound curb weight. The loss of 360 pounds of performance-robbing weight was welcomed by Camaro enthusiasts, given that the 350-cubic-inch LM1 V-8 would no longer be available in the Camaro. The largest engine available when the third-generation car debuted was a 305-cubic-inch V-8. The carbureted LG4 version of this engine had been available the previous year, though it had generated 20 more horsepower in 1981: 165 horsepower versus 145 in 1982. The LU5 version of the engine, available only as a $450 option on the Z28, used a throttle-body fuel injection (TBI) system to generate the same 165 horsepower as the carbureted engine of the previous year, though torque was down to 240 lb-ft from the 245 lb-ft the carbureted LG4 had pumped out in 1981.

The biggest change in the Camaro's engine stable occurred at the opposite end of the performance spectrum. The base engine was no longer a six-cylinder; Chevrolet borrowed the 151-cubic-inch Iron Duke four-cylinder from Pontiac Division and made it the standard engine in the Camaro Sport Coupe. This engine developed 90 horsepower and 134 lb-ft of torque.

For $8,029.50, the most miserly Camaro buyers got a car powered by the Iron Duke hitched to a four-speed manual transmission, which was the standard transmission on all 1982 Camaros. For $125 more, he or she could upgrade to the 102-horsepower, 173-cubic-inch V-6 that came standard in the $9,665.06 Berlinetta Coupe. It cost a Sport Coupe buyer $295 to upgrade to the LG4 engine, though a Berlinetta buyer could make the same upgrade for just $170. Neither buyer could get the optional LU5 engine available on the Z28, which had a base price of $10,099.

Picking up the Pace

The Camaro once again earned the honor of pacing the Indianapolis 500 in 1982, and once again Chevrolet capitalized on this by offering a pace car replica edition of the Z28 Camaro. Chevrolet sold 6,360 of these handsome silver-and-blue pace car editions at $10,999 apiece.

This contributed to a total output of 189,742 Camaros for the 1982 model year. While still nowhere near the record output of just three years earlier, it still represented a nearly 50 percent increase over the previous year. This is especially impressive given that, like the 1970 car, the 1982 Camaro was a late-release model, debuting in February 1982 instead of the previous fall. There was more good news: Z28 sales shot up to 71,242 cars, the second-best year yet for the sportiest Camaro model. In a grim period for the American auto industry, the 1982 Camaro was Chevrolet's hottest-selling car. Best of all, the Camaro absolutely smoked Ford's Mustang, which sold a paltry 130,418 units for the 1982 model year.

Always the first choice of enthusiasts, a manual transmission allows increased control during spirited driving. A beefy ball topped the five-speed shifter in the 1984 Z28.

Even though the Mustang was still a fairly new design, it needed some help. When the Mustang had been redesigned in 1979, Ford based the protopony car on its Fox platform, the basic underpinning of such cars as the Ford Fairmont Futura. When any amount of power was applied to this chassis, the rear end would hop like a 1962 Chevy II. When compared to the relatively sophisticated chassis on the new Camaro, the original Fox-based Mustang was hopelessly outclassed.

For 1982, Ford revived the Mustang GT and along with it the 302-cubic-inch V-8 engine, now producing 157 horsepower. Thanks to the Camaro's additional 300 pounds of weight, the Mustang could hold its own against the Camaro in straight-line acceleration. *Car and Driver* wrote: "[Chevrolet's] 165-hp throttle-body fuel injection wasn't enough to keep the overweight Z28 from getting sand kicked in its face by the Mustang at the stoplights." Throw a curve into the road, however, and the nimble Camaro would leave the Mustang for dead.

Horsepower Wars Heat Up

For 1983, Ford mounted a Holley four-barrel carburetor to the Mustang GT's 302 and bumped power up to 175, enough to handily outrun the LU5 Z28–powered Z28, which also generated 175 horsepower in 1983. But Chevrolet had something even better planned for 1983: the 305-cubic-inch L69, or rather the 5.0 HO, since like Ford and Pontiac, Chevrolet had adopted the technique of labeling its engines according to cubic liters rather than cubic inches.

Chevrolet adopted traditional hot-rodding techniques, such as freer-breathing exhaust pipes and better-flowing air intakes, to extract 25 additional horsepower from the 5-liter engine. The 5.0 HO borrowed a sharper-opening, longer-duration camshaft from the Corvette's 350-cubic-inch L83 engine, but most importantly, Chevy engineers ditched the restrictive TBI system and mounted a Rochester four-barrel carburetor on top of the engine, bumping output to 190 horsepower.

To capitalize on the Z28's newfound muscle, Chevrolet engineers gave the car a standard Borg-Warner T-5 five-speed manual transmission, the only transmission available with an L69-equipped Z28. The L69 powertrain significantly boosted performance, allowing *Road & Track* testers to push the car through the quarter-mile 0.8 seconds quicker than an LU5-equipped car. *Car and Driver* magazine, which published a comparison test between the Z28 and Mustang GT in its June 1983 issue, ran an L69 Z28 through the quarter-mile in 15 seconds flat, making it the quickest Camaro the magazine had tested in a generation. In comparison, the Mustang's generated a 15.4-second time, which was still quicker than most other cars sold at the time, including Chevrolet's Corvette sports car.

The Camaro maintained a slight edge over the Mustang in outright acceleration, but it humiliated the Ford on a slalom course. "The Z28 simply dominated the event," the magazine reported, "averaging a speed of 60.6 mph versus the Mustang's 57.9 mph. The Camaro carves its way from gate to gate; it changes direction completely and without hesitation, just like a race car. You just steer; the car does the rest. In contrast, the Mustang slithers through the gates, heeling over onto its outside front tire and understeering from one corner to the next."

The Camaro's dominance continued when *Car and Driver* tested the cars at Willow Springs Raceway:

As speeds increase, the Mustang gets worse and the Camaro gets better. The Ford skates into turns, reminding you of its limited 0.76-g capability on the skid pad. The inability to heel-and-toe makes approaches to slow corners exciting, while the lifeless steering makes it impossible to check the sliding rear tires with any predictability. In slow- and medium-speed right-handers, the Mustang's dreaded rear-axle hop raises its ugly head, and in left-handers the rear tires try to beat you to the exit. In comparison, the Camaro feels the same as before, only faster. It plunges into a corner far harder than the Mustang, front and rear tires working in close-coupled harmony, its 0.83-g capability conserving the momentum gathered on the straight. The Z28 is the closest thing to a race car built on an American assembly line, closer even than the Corvette.

In an effort to keep the driver and passengers from sliding around in their seats during hard cornering, side bolsters and nonslip materials were used in the 1984 Z28. Per Camaro tradition, the rear seats were a painful place to spend significant amounts of time.

Quality Control Problems

The Camaro was beating the Mustang every time it went up against the Ford in a comparison test, and it was beating the Mustang in the market. Chevrolet sold 154,381 Camaros in 1983 versus Ford's 120,873 Mustangs, but both Ford and Chevrolet saw sales drop from 1982 to 1983. In fact, the Mustang's performance in the marketplace marked its most dismal sales year in the car's 20-year history.

Part of the problem was that the United States was just emerging from a long recession, and the economy had yet to pick up measurable momentum. The American car-buying public's increasing tendency to choose the excellent cars coming from Japan over the offerings from Detroit added to the overall dismal state of the U.S. auto industry.

Camaro sales weren't helped by the new cars' growing reputation for quality-control problems. When *Car and Driver* concluded a long-term test of a 1982 Z28, as reported in the magazine's December 1983 issue, it described the experience as "a 25,000-mile tale of woe." The problems started from the day the car was delivered and editors examined the paint on the car, which they described as "atrocious." The automatic transmission balked at shifting into reverse and upshifting, a problem Chevrolet service people were never able to solve properly. At 11,700 miles, the transmission gave up the ghost and was replaced. Several thousand miles later, the differential started to disintegrate, followed by a complete failure of the engine-management computer. The rear suspension was rebuilt, and the computer replaced at 20,000 miles, but the troubles didn't stop there. After another 5,338 miles of failure after failure, the magazine decided to end the test early and return the car to Chevrolet.

More for show than function, the rear spoiler on the 1984 Z28 imparted a serious visual note to the overall serious look to the Chevrolet pony car. Handsome wraparound taillights were an elegant yet simple solution to the question of how to incorporate side marker lights into the vehicle design.

The car the magazine tested was clearly a lemon and may not have been indicative of overall Camaro quality, but enough buyers experienced at least some of the problems the test car exhibited to dampen second-year sales. Chevrolet wasted no time in addressing these problems, and by 1984, the Camaro was a much-improved car.

Berlinetta Hits the Big Time

Chevrolet made some revisions to the rear suspension and axle in order to cure the problems that plagued early third-generation Camaros. In addition to getting a better handle on quality-control problems, Chevrolet refined the entire Camaro lineup for 1984, tweaking suspension bushings and settings in order to find a better compromise between performance and comfort. These relatively minor changes produced results that exceeded everyone's expectations. *Car and Driver* wrote:

> Chevrolet has followed through with a host of improvements during the two years of Z28 production: the rear axle has been totally redesigned, a five-speed option has been added, the ill-conceived throttle-body fuel injection has been dumped, the engine is smoother and more powerful, and the ride is drastically improved. What's more, the Z28's handling didn't suffer while its chassis was being refined. This is still the closest thing to race car responsiveness you can buy off the showroom floor.

Next page: Riding on 16x8-inch cast-aluminum wheels, the 1985 IROC-Z stuffed Goodyear Eagle P245/50VR rubber inside the wheelwells. All of the engine's cooling air came from beneath the front air dam, improving the vehicle's aerodynamics.

The colorful Z28 IROC-Z emblem, mounted on the passenger side of the dashboard, made its debut in 1985. The IROC Sport Equipment Package, RPO B4Z, was a $659 option.

The biggest changes to the Camaro line in 1984 were bestowed upon the Berlinetta model. Since its 1982 redesign, the Berlinetta had been the slowest-selling Camaro model. Chevrolet marketed this upscale Camaro, which featured almost every available option as standard equipment, as a luxury sport coupe to compete with cars like Ford's Thunderbird.

For 1984, Chevrolet's stylists redesigned the interior of the Berlinetta, swathing the seats and door panels in striped velour cloth, putting folding seats in back to help maximize the limited interior space, and mounting a new instrument panel that included new center and overhead consoles. They placed switchgear in pods on either side of the steering wheel; between them sat a new digital speedometer and an electronic bargraph tachometer. This was in keeping with the trends set by many of the Japanese sport coupes of the era. The base engine was the 107-horsepower LC1 V-6, but an LG4 V-8 was available for an extra $375. A three-speed automatic transmission was standard, with a four-speed automatic transmission a $295 option. Chevrolet didn't offer a manual transmission for the 1984 Berlinetta.

When *Motor Trend* tabulated the costs of all the bells and whistles on the Berlinetta it tested for its May 1984 issue, the base price of $10,895 transmogrified into an as-tested price of $13,723.

The Handling Wars Begin

In its May 1984 issue, *Car and Driver* published a test that pitted five American cars with sporting pretense against one another to determine which car handled the best. The editors selected the Z28 over the Trans Am because their prior testing had already proven that the Camaro did indeed out-handle its brother from Pontiac. Instead of the Trans Am, the editors selected Pontiac's new Fiero as that division's representative in the fight. Rounding out the test were Chevrolet's new fourth-generation Corvette, Dodge's Daytona Turbo Z (the only front-wheel-drive entrant in the melee), and Ford's latest, greatest version of the Mustang, the SVO.

In its first year, the Z28 IROC-Z option was popular, with 18,418 units sold. It was not a solo model but rather an option in the Z28 line.

Ford's engineers had been working hard to solve the Mustang's handling issues. In 1984, Ford's Special Vehicle Operations (SVO) team made great strides toward taming rear-wheel hop when it introduced a revised rear suspension for the Mustang. This system used four shocks instead of two to control axle hop. Initially, the SVO team mounted this new suspension on the Mustang SVO, which used a high-tech turbocharged four-cylinder engine that matched the 175-horsepower output of the 5.0-liter Mustang GT.

On paper, the Corvette should have walked away from the crowd in this contest. It generated the highest skid pad numbers, had the most sophisticated suspension, and had the largest engine of the group, as well as the best power-to-weight ratio. Likewise, the SVO, with its radically redesigned suspension, should have been a contender, but it was the Camaro that came out on top. The magazine described the car as "a delightful combination of tight adhesion, telegraphic controls, manageable response, and forgiving limits. We are pleased to report that Chevrolet's once-rough gem has been polished into a handling jewel."

The editors at *Car and Driver* weren't the only people impressed by the refined Camaro. Sales increased to 261,591 units for the 1984 model year, marking the third best year in Camaro sales history. The Z28 model fared even better, selling 100,899 units, making 1984 the best year ever for Z28 sales.

IROC-Z

The International Race of Champions had been on a hiatus between 1981 and 1983, but it returned in 1984, once again pitting drivers from all racing disciplines against one another in identically prepared Camaros. Having had terrific sales success with its 1982 Indianapolis 500 pace car replica series, Chevrolet decided to capitalize on its racing connections once more and market a car to commemorate the International Race of Champions: the IROC-Z.

The IROC-Z wasn't a separate model, but rather a $659 option package (RPO B4Z) for the Z28 model. This was much more than a simple trim package. The entire chassis was stiffened with a crossmember that Chevrolet's designers referred to as the "wonder bar." A modified suspension—special front struts, springs, and jounce bumpers, Delco-Bilstein rear shocks, recalibrated rear springs, and a stronger rear stabilizer bar—lowered the ride height by a half-inch and improved the handling of what was already the best-handling car in America. The tires deserve a portion of the credit for the car's improved handling. While the base four-cylinder Sport Coupe still used old-fashioned 14-inch wheels, the IROC-Z used 16-inch rims, covered with the same P245/50VR-16 Goodyear Eagle VR50s found on the Corvette.

If the buyer selected the standard five-speed transmission, the strongest engine he or she could order was the 190-horsepower L69 ($680). If the buyer selected the optional ($395) four-speed automatic, he or she could fork over another $680 and order the new 305-cubic-inch LB9 V-8. Like the earlier LU5, the LB9 featured fuel injection, though in this case it was a modern port-type system rather than the crude

throttle-body system used in the earlier car. The system, which Chevrolet named "Tuned Port Injection," used long, curved intake runners that smoothed out the power-band, creating tractable power that peaked at 215 horsepower at 4,400 rpm and 275 lb-ft of torque at 2,800 rpm. This was too much torque for the Borg-Warner five-speed transmission, necessitating the use of a four-speed automatic.

The Z28 benefited from a nose job in 1985, a change made more obvious on the IROC-Z, thanks to the car's handsome monochromatic paint job. Striking striped seats with "CAMARO" script repeated on them finally had foam in the right places instead of the wrong places; this was the first Camaro in history not to be panned for uncomfortable seats.

Car and Driver tested both an automatic-equipped LB9 version and a manual L69 version of the IROC-Z for its October 1984 issue and came away impressed. The editors called the LB9 engine "a gem," though they weren't terribly impressed with the shift points

RPO LB9 was an optional tuned-port fuel-injected 305-cubic-inch V-8 rated at 215 horsepower, but it was only available with an automatic transmission. The Camaro shared induction technology with the Corvette.

Chevrolet's engineers raised the Z28's performance and handling envelope in 1985 with the introduction of the IROC-Z. With its sticky Goodyear Gatorbacks and Delco front struts incorporating special valving and Bilstein shock absorbers, it was one of the finest handling automobiles on American roads in the mid-1980s.

on the automatic transmission. "Unfortunately, the automatic gets all confused around town," editor Rich Ceppos wrote. "Its constant cycling is nothing short of annoying."

When *Motor Trend* compared a 1985 IROC-Z to a 1985 Mustang SVO, which by that time was cranking out 205 horsepower from its boosted four-cylinder engine, it chose an L69 five-speed car over the injected LB9 and its required automatic. "It's not that the four-speed automatic is a bad transmission. It simply does not offer a comparable—or compatible—level of performance to the fuel-injected LB9," the magazine reported. "The engine deserves better."

Regardless of what testers thought of the automatic transmission, professional pundits realized that the IROC-Z was a special car. *Car and Driver* picked it as one of the magazine's 10-best cars for 1985, writing: "There can be no denying that the IROC Z28 does get the job done. It is very fast and very good at all the things we expect sports coupes to do . . . The Camaro looks like a hundred-thousand-dollar car, and if we saw the Camaro as seldom as we see Ferraris, we'd probably pay that for it."

A Year of Reduction

Chevrolet also applied the new fuel-injection technology to the six-cylinder engine, bumping power to 135 horsepower, and made it the base Berlinetta engine. This boosted Berlinetta performance but did little to inflate flagging sales. Few people seemed enamored of the Berlinetta and its Atari-inspired video-game dash. When *Car and Driver* compared eight sport coupes in its May 1985 issue, the Berlinetta came in dead last. In 1986, the Berlinetta accounted for just two percent of Camaro sales. The model was discontinued early in the 1986 model year, replaced by the LT option package that became available for the Sport Coupe in 1987; or rather, it was replaced by four different LT option packages, ranging in price from $1,522 to $2,858, depending on the level of equipment.

In general, 1986 was a year of reduction for the Camaro. The four-cylinder Iron Duke continued to be listed as the base engine in the Sport Coupe, but no cars seem to have been equipped with this engine in 1986. The LB9 engine lost 25 horsepower, falling to the same 190 horsepower output as the L69. The LB9 did gain 10 lb-ft of torque, though. Chevrolet also gained sales. After falling to 180,018 units for 1985, Camaro sales rose to 192,219 units for 1986. Z28 sales, including IROC-Z versions, had fallen to 68,403 units in 1985 but rose back to 88,132 units in 1986, making it the second best year ever for Chevrolet's Z car.

Meanwhile, the folks at Dearborn hadn't been sitting around with their thumbs buried in their lower intestinal tracts. For 1985, Ford bumped the high-output version of the 5.0 engine to 210 horsepower, which was enough to make the lighter Mustang show its taillights to even the LB9 Camaro in a stoplight drag race. The advantage the Camaro had previously held in the slalom narrowed too, thanks to the adoption of the four-shock SVO rear suspension system. Many testers attributed the IROC-Z's better road-holding numbers to its huge Goodyear tires.

Per the fashion of the time, the interior of the 1985 IROC-Z was all crisp lines and somber tones. Some viewed it as austere, while others called it professional.

This improved performance helped Ford once again pass Chevrolet in pony car sales. Mustang sales had rebounded from the low point in 1983 and, in 1986, climbed back up to 224,410 units, indicating that the U.S. auto market still placed a high premium on the ability to win a stoplight drag race.

Return of the 350

For serious Camaro fans, 1986 was a year of waiting for the long-rumored return of the 350-cubic-inch small-block V-8 that had made its first appearance in the original Camaro SS350. The press expected the 350 to return for the 1986 model year, thinking it unlikely that Chevrolet wouldn't respond to the Mustang's newfound muscle, and Chevrolet was more than happy to oblige, but development problems meant that the 350 wouldn't be ready in time for the 1986 model year.

For 1987, IROC-Z buyers could finally order RPO B2L, a $1,045 option that netted them a 225-horsepower 350-cubic-inch (or 5.7-liter, in the new metric vernacular) V-8 generating 330 lb-ft of torque. To create the B2L, Chevy engineers took the L89 engine from the Corvette, replaced the L89 aluminum heads with cast-iron units, and bolted on a pair of cast-iron manifolds in place of the stainless-steel tubular headers from the L89. They had to do this to fit the 5.7 engine in the Camaro's engine bay, and the change was the primary culprit responsible for the B2L's 15-horsepower decrease from the L89.

This engine put the Camaro's performance back on par with the Mustang, which by then was generating 225 horsepower from its 5.0 engine, but the Mustang still had an edge when it came to transmissions. Ford offered a five-speed manual for the Mustang

Vibrant seat covers carried over the red and black interior theme of the 1985 IROC-Z. Engineers fitted the catalytic converter beneath the raised portion of the floor in front of the passenger seat.

GT, while Chevrolet still did not have a manual capable of handling the torque output of the B2L. Chevrolet did give the four-speed slush box the Corvette's torque converter, which had its shift points recalibrated to better suit the power curve of the 5.7-liter engine.

While Chevrolet continued to add amenities like leather seating surfaces to the option sheet, the B2L contained one mandatory option delete that drove away a huge number of potential customers: air conditioning. By 1987, only the most lowly economy cars failed to include air conditioning. Even most Chevrolet Cavaliers were air-conditioned.

Return of the Ragtop

While a buyer couldn't get factory air conditioning on a 5.7-liter IROC-Z in 1987, he or she could get natural air conditioning in the form of a folding cloth top. For the first

Unique to the IROC-Z were the front fog lamps, a 15-millimeter lowered ride height, special exterior graphics, and power steering modified to increase road feel.

Unlike the 5-mile-per-hour bumpers on earlier Camaros, the 1985 IROC-Z's bumper caps were well integrated into the exterior design. This was the last year that did not incorporate a center high-mounted stop light (CHMSL).

time in almost two decades, Chevrolet offered a convertible version of the Camaro. Chevrolet shipped completed T-top cars to a company called American Specialty Company (ASC) in Southgate, Michigan, where ASC's technicians began cutting and welding and installing chassis-stiffening hardware, ultimately producing a convertible Camaro. Chevrolet used T-top cars because they already had extra bracing installed at the factory.

All this mucking about with torches and welders didn't come cheap. The Camaro Sport Coupe Convertible listed for $15,208, $4,799 more than the regular Sport Coupe. The Z28 Convertible started at $17,632. Throw in $500 worth of performance options, the $699 Base IROC Group, the $1,045 B2L engine and its prerequisite $490 automatic transmission, the $3,273 IROC Option Package 3, and a buyer was looking at a car pushing the $30,000 mark, and maybe more if dealer markup was factored in.

Car and Driver tested a 1987 Z28 convertible in its October 1986 issue, calling the car "a particularly good example" of the convertible breed. "This is a car destined to instill genuine automotive lust in the hearts of anyone lucky enough to see one, let alone drive one." They found the car to be as rigid and well mannered as most other convertibles, and were impressed with the quality of the top mechanism and the clean execution of the conversion.

In 1987, Chevrolet offered the widest and wildest selection of Camaros that the company had produced since 1969, but sales declined, falling to 137,760 units. Ford once again sold more Mustangs than Chevrolet sold Camaros. The Camaro still

5.7 TUNED PORT INJECTION

The big Camaro news for the 1987 IROC-Z was the introduction of the 5.7-liter V-8. Rated at 225 horsepower, it was sourced from the Corvette, but in the Camaro it used iron heads and exhaust manifolds. In the Corvette, the engine delivered 240 horsepower.

impressed magazine testers—*Road & Track* picked the IROC-Z over the Mustang GT when price was not factored into the equation—but for most buyers, price was factored into the equation. The decked-out Mustang the magazine tested cost just $12,548, less than the $12,675 base price of the Z-28. The full-zoot IROC-Z with the B2L engine tested by the magazine cost $18,179. For that price, there was still no air conditioning, while the less-expensive Mustang had air and a five-speed transmission. The Mustang matched the Camaro in quarter-mile times—each car ran through the traps in 15.3 seconds—and beat the Camaro in the slalom, usurping the Camaro's handling crown.

The Mini Death and Rebirth of the Z28

Because Chevrolet was focused on developing a replacement for the Camaro, the division invested very little money or effort in changing the car during the final five years of third-generation production. Horsepower levels went up and down but mostly up, as engine options proliferated into a bewildering array of alphanumeric nomenclature. The B2L grew to 230 horsepower in 1988, and jumped again in 1991, up to 245 horsepower. In 1992, B2L torque jumped from 330 lb-ft to 345 lb-ft. LB9 horsepower rose to 220 horsepower in 1988, fell to 210 horsepower in 1991, but jumped back to 230 horsepower in 1992, the last year of production for the third-generation car.

The array of models in the Camaro lineup became almost as confusing as the engines powering them. In 1988, the Z28 once again disappeared. The IROC-Z had proven so popular that it became the performance version of the Camaro, but when the International Race of Champions series switched to Dodge Daytonas in 1990, Chevrolet lost the rights to the name and had to switch back to Z28.

In 1989, Chevrolet added a new RS trim package, which combined the sporty appearance of an IROC-Z with the base Sport Coupe mechanicals. The RS featured

body-colored front, side, and rear ground effects, a spoiler, and 15-inch body-colored aluminum five-spoke wheels. The base engine for the RS was the V-6 that now produced 135 horsepower and 160 lb-ft of torque, but Chevrolet offered a 170-horsepower V-8 as an option. RS buyers were denied the LB9 and B2L V-8s, which were restricted to the IROC-Z.

Chevrolet developed the RS package with help from employees at the Camaro assembly plant in Van Nuys, California. The division test-marketed the RS in California

Chevrolet color-keyed the cast-aluminum wheels to the body color on the 1987 IROC-Z. Deeply inset headlights lent an aggressive face to the 2+2 pony car, now pitted in a sales race with Ford's Mustang.

(the car's intended geographic market, leading to the RS being known internally as the "California Camaro") in 1987 and 1988, and the car struck a chord with buyers. In 1989, the RS replaced the Sport Coupe as the base Camaro model.

A New Kind of COPO

As had happened in the past, racing drove the most interesting development in the final years of the third-generation Camaro. The SCCA had developed the popular

Showroom Stock racing class, a class that proved a perfect place to highlight the Camaro's performance. It also highlighted the Camaro's weaknesses, since the rules precluded major suspension changes beyond shocks, struts, wheels, and tires.

Phil Minch, a GM brake engineer, Chuck Hughes, chief engineer for the Camaro platform, and Ray Canales, powertrain manager for GM's F-bodies, conspired to produce a back-door racer support program in the tradition of Vince Piggins' COPO program.

The team grew in size and in scope, producing a comprehensive racing package that included a lower fifth-gear ratio, an aluminum driveshaft, and an oil cooler, among other parts. They labeled this option "1LE," but it was not an option a buyer could order in the conventional sense. Ordering it was more akin to knowing a secret handshake. To get the 1LE package, the buyer had to check the right combination of option boxes. First, he or she had to order the G92 Performance Axle option and not order air conditioning. Then the buyer had to select the LB9 with the five-speed manual transmission or the B2L with the automatic. When this was all done in the proper order, it triggered the 1LE option code.

When equipped with the 1LE/G92 package, the 5-liter LB9 engine cranked out 230 horsepower and 300 lb-ft of torque, nearly matching the output of the larger 5.7 B2L engine. *Motor Trend* tested a 1LE/LB9 car and turned in a quarter-mile time of 14.8 seconds.

Chevrolet first started offering this package in mid-1988, but few people knew of its existence. The division filled four properly checked order forms in 1988, none in 1989, and 62 in 1990. But after being trounced by 1LE Camaros, racers began to catch on to this incredible bargain and orders picked up, jumping to 478 in 1991 and 705 in 1992. The fact that sharp Camaro enthusiasts had figured out the system and began ordering 1LE cars for street use also contributed to the jump in sales.

Clever buyers who wanted the performance of the 1LE package but wanted it in a more civilized car with air conditioning—and who were adept at negotiating the political minefield of Chevrolet's option sheet—could order RPO B4C, available in 1991 and 1992. This provided most of the best pieces of the 1LE package, including the 145-mile-per-hour speedometer, but to get it, the buyer needed a sympathetic dealer; RPO B4C was a package for police cars and was not intended to be sold to the public. It was also only available on RS Coupes. Chevrolet built 592 B4C Camaros in 1991 and 589 in 1992. Most of these went to police departments, but a few ended up being sold to private buyers as street cars.

Twenty-Five Years

In 1992, Chevrolet celebrated 25 years of Camaro production. All 1992 Camaros had 25th anniversary emblems on their instrument panels, and all could be ordered with the RPO Z03 Heritage Package, consisting of special stripes and paint.

Chevrolet may have celebrated the Camaro's silver anniversary in 1992, but many Camaro fans within General Motors worried about the car's survival. While the final versions of the third-generation Camaro were better cars than ever, its future in Chevrolet's lineup was, as always, uncertain. Sales bounced around as much during that period as did horsepower ratings, going up and down, but mostly down. Sales fell to 96,275 units in 1988, bounced up to 110,739 in 1989, then plummeted to 34,986 in 1990, when another UAW strike crippled Camaro production, though the loss of the IROC-Z moniker and the ill-conceived death of the Z28 nameplate hadn't helped the situation. Sales rebounded to 101,316 in 1991 but fell to 70,712 in 1992, the final year of the third generation's lifespan.

Sales may have fluctuated during the final two years of the third generation's lifespan, but the quality of the car improved dramatically in 1991 and 1992. New assembley methods and welding techniques greatly enhanced structural rigidity during those final two years of production, leadng to vastly improved cars. Another thing that remained constant was the steady increase in prices; by the time the third-generation Camaro gave way to the fourth generation, the base price of a convertible Z28 had risen to $21,500. Another constant was performance: the third-generation Camaro may have been in production for 11 years and almost as long in tooth as its predecessor had been at the beginning of the previous decade, but it was still one of the fastest, best-handling cars sold in America.

By 1988, the IROC-Z had become a stand-alone model Camaro, and the Z28 name was pulled. Handsome aluminum wheels were part of the package in 1990.

CHAPTER FIVE

THE LAST CAMARO?

Yet again, a Camaro Z28 found itself in front of a hoard of open-wheel race cars as it paced the 1993 Indianapolis 500. Eschewing simple stripes, the pace car edition wore vibrant, flowing multi-colored bands down the side, making the vehicle appear in motion while sitting still.

For 1993, Chevrolet introduced yet another new Camaro. While the third-generation car had survived attempts to convert the Camaro platform to front-wheel-drive, it looked very much like the fourth-generation version would funnel its power to the pavement via the front wheels. For the fourth generation of F-bodies, the front-wheel-drive program, internally coded "GM80," advanced much further in development before being saved from that shameful fate. The GM80 F-bodies were to be relatively powerful front-wheel-drive cars with low curb weights, thanks to Saturn-like plastic bodies.

The Camaro's sinking sales actually saved the car from becoming just another front-wheel-drive econo-crapbox. Money was tight in the late 1980s. The U.S. auto industry continued to lose market share to the Japanese. In the middle of the decade, General Motors invested a great deal of money launching the Saturn brand in an attempt to meet the Japanese head on. There just wasn't a lot of money available to

Above: Chevrolet was never one to shy away from telling the world that its cars were pacing the greatest spectacle in racing. The 1993 Z28 pace car replica was no exception, as eye-catching decals were festooned on the front fenders and doors.

Left: Colored stripes in the interior echoed the exterior paint scheme, including the black/white treatment. The dashboard and instrument panel featured soft curves, following the trend at the time for organic shapes surrounding the vehicle's occupants. The rear seats were still no place for an adult.

The fourth-generation Camaro was strictly a bottom-breather. Like its Corvette cousin, all cooling and induction air was ingested beneath the nose of the car, allowing the aerodynamic engineers to shape the nose to be as slippery as possible in the pursuit of improved fuel economy.

develop a front-wheel-drive Camaro. Chevrolet could have resorted to parts-bin engineering and badged the coupe version of its upcoming front-wheel-drive Lumina as a Camaro, but making that platform worthy of the name "Camaro" would have been costly, and the sales potential of such a car wouldn't justify the expense. The Camaro design team took too much pride in its world-beating sports coupe to simply glue a "Z28" badge onto a two-door Lumina. They'd leave that ignominy to the Monte Carlo development team.

Ford had already tried converting an iconic American sporty car to front-wheel-drive when it developed a front-wheel-drive version of the Mustang. The public's

resistance to a front-wheel-drive Mustang proved so strong that the company renamed car, which had already been developed, the "Probe" and sold the poor, unwanted thing alongside the Mustang. The traditional rear-wheel-drive Mustang remained in Ford's lineup, while the Probe disappeared. Though the Probe's failure to find a sustainable customer base may have stemmed in part from the fact that it shared its name with an infamous sexual novelty device, for the most part it reinforced the notion that fans of American performance cars preferred the handling dynamics of rear-wheel-drive vehicles.

In 1989, after witnessing the Probe's lukewarm reception in the marketplace, General Motors pulled the plug on the GM80 project, saving the Camaro from becoming

Servicing a fourth-generation Camaro was a task best left to professionals. The rear half of the LT1 5.7-liter engine is under the windshield, making access difficult. Note the location of the windshield washer reservoir, in front of the radiator. The engineers had to be creative in placing components.

Each 1993 Indianapolis 500 pace car replica wore a special badge on the nose commemorating the event. Dimples in the bumper cover were for the mounting of front license plates in states that require them.

a bloated Saturn coupe. *Sports Car International* summed up the wisdom of this decision when it tested a Z28 for its May 1993 issue: "Give the Japanese their four-cylinder, front-wheel-drive sport coupes. For V-8s with big torque and acceleration, Detroit is still the only game around." In reality, the bean counters killed the GM80 program, which was so far over budget that the program would have lost untold millions for GM, but it was the Camaro enthusiast who benefitted from this failure.

Longer, Wider, Sleeker

The new car kept a rear-wheel-drive configuration, but it did adopt plastic body panels developed for the GM80 project. In addition to the plastic front and rear fascias, the 1993 Camaro featured reaction injection-molded plastic fenders and sheet-molded compound plastic panels for the doors, roof, and rear hatch.

The nose on the 1993 Z28 Indy 500 pace car is the road-going version of a shark on wheels. Within the long prow of the Camaro is the radiator. Side marker lights were smoothly integrated into the curvaceous design.

Even with plastic body panels, the new Camaro was heavier than its predecessor—the base six-cylinder coupe weighed 3,241 pounds, while the 1992 six-cylinder RS had weighed 3,060 pounds—because the new car was bigger in almost every dimension. The wheelbase remained virtually unchanged—the floor stamping was basically carried over from 1992—but the car was 0.5 inch longer and 1.7 inches wider. The look of the new car changed much more dramatically than these numbers would indicate, thanks in large part to a new, swept-back windshield rake of 68 degrees, which gave the Camaro a sleek stance similar to that of many of the sport coupes coming from Japan and Europe at the time.

The live-axle rear suspension carried over from 1992; though the press had been mewling for an independent rear suspension since the introduction of the 1967 Camaro, the solid-axle setup still worked extremely well. Chevrolet finally did give the Camaro a much-needed rack-and-pinion steering system up front, making an already-excellent-handling car even better. Camaro chassis engineers ditched the MacPherson struts in favor of a more modern short-long-arm front suspension design and created a stiffer body. "The body structure is amazingly solid compared with the previous generation," *Car and Driver* wrote of the 1993 Z28, "an improvement that gives a quality feel by eliminating creaks and squeaks."

Road & Track echoed this sentiment, saying the rigid chassis "would probably do any Mercedes-Benz or BMW structural engineer proud."

The suspension improvements and more rigid chassis brought Camaro handling to a new level of excellence. "It doesn't oversteer as much as the old Camaro, so the Z28

The flow of the sheet metal continued to the rear, where a graceful spoiler spanned the huge rear window. Instead of a stylistically clumsy housing for the center-mounted brake light, the Camaro's designers placed the light within the rear spoiler without marring the overall design.

doesn't feel as out of control when you're tossing it around," Jean Lindamood wrote when she tested a Z28 for the January 1993 issue of *Automobile*. "The overall feel is tauter, more controlled."

To capitalize on this rigid new body, all versions of the car rode on 16-inch wheels. On the Z28, these rims were covered with massive 235/55R16 tires. Even bigger 245/50ZR rubber was available as a $225 option. Four-wheel power disc brakes, previously available only as part of the 1LE Performance Package, came as standard equipment on all models. Drum brakes had officially gone the way of the carburetor, manual choke, and side-vent window.

The 1LE option returned, again triggered by ordering the G92 performance axle without ordering air conditioning. Since the Z28 was so vastly improved over the previous car, it didn't need as many Band-Aid cures as the previous 1LE package offered. The new 1LE package no longer featured such high-tech equipment as an aluminum

driveshaft, but it still included quite a few high-performance suspension bits, and the car was still best suited for a racetrack. Chevrolet built 19 1LE cars in 1993, 135 in 1994, 106 in 1995, 55 in 1996, 48 in 1997, 99 in 1998, and 74 in 1999. In 2000, oursourced 1LE production to SLP and the package was no longer a regular production option.

After being criticized for the convoluted lineup of models and engine options offered in previous years, Chevrolet kept it simple with the new Camaro and only offered the car in two versions for 1993: base Sport Coupe and Z28. The convertible was absent from the lineup but reappeared for the 1994 model year. By that time, coupes and convertibles would be built in the same assembly plant. Chevrolet no longer had ASC chop the tops off coupes to create convertibles, though the California firm still supplied the high-quality hardware for the folding top.

For the first time, Camaro assembly no longer took place in the United States; starting in 1993, Chevrolet produced all Camaros at GM's Sainte Therese facility near Montreal, Quebec. This completely refurbished factory would play a major role in

Artist David Kimble was afforded access to the new 1993 Camaro long before the public saw the car to allow him to research the vehicle for his phantom rendering. *General Motors Corp. Used with permission, GM Media Archives*

improving the Camaro's reputation for quality control, which had suffered during the previous generation's 11-year production run.

New Generation Power

Chevrolet designers produced one of the boldest automotive designs in recent generations with the 1993 Camaro. Some fans liked its innovative style while others thought it strayed too far from the traditional Camaro look, but most fans agreed it was a distinctive and attractive car.

Likewise, no one could complain about the powertrain options. The V-6 engine had grown to 3.4 liters and generated 160 horsepower and 200 lb-ft of torque, making it stronger than some of the V-8s from the Camaro's dark ages. *Road & Track* tested a Sport Coupe with a V-6 for its July 1993 issue and managed a 16.6-second quarter-mile, nearly equaling the 16.0-second quarter-mile time that *Car and Driver* recorded when it tested a 1982 Z28.

But the biggest Camaro news lurked in the engine compartment of the new Z28, which housed a version of Chevrolet's LT1 350-cubic-inch small-block V-8. The LT1

had debuted in the 1992 Corvette, the result of Chevrolet's engineers completely rethinking the small-block V-8 concept, and had a net power rating higher than the gross power rating of most small-block 350s from the pre-emissions era. In the Corvette, this engine generated 300 horsepower and 330 lb-ft of torque, putting it on par with its namesake—the 1970 LT1—when the different measuring techniques were factored in.

The LT1 generated 275 horsepower and 325 lb-ft of torque in the Camaro, primarily because of a more restrictive exhaust system used on the Camaro. Camaro's engine team made a few other alterations to the LT1, mostly cost-saving measures such as substituting two-bolt main bearings rather than the four-bolt system used on the Corvette. Even with a 25-horsepower loss, the new LT1 made the 1993 Z28 one of the most powerful Camaros that Chevrolet had ever built.

The new Z28 came with a Borg-Warner T56 six-speed manual—the same gearbox found in the exotic, expensive Dodge Viper sports car—as its standard transmission. The Sport Coupe came with a five-speed manual, and both versions could be had with a four-speed automatic for an additional $595.

Next page: Contrasting exterior mirrors and roof gave the visual illusion that the 1993 Camaro Z28 sat lower than the previous car; in reality, the car was taller.

The six-speed tranny and LT1 engine were only available on the Z28, but once again, clever customers with sympathetic dealers could find an exception: Special Service Package RPO B4C designed for police use. For $3,335 above the $13,399 sticker price of a Sport Coupe, a buyer could get a six-speed, LT1-powered Sport Coupe with a heavy-duty suspension ($3,885 with automatic transmission). This priced the car almost exactly at the Z28's $16,799 sticker, so for 1993, RPO B4C amounted to a Z28 without the flashy graphics, which had a certain appeal. "When the local deputy sheriff knows you as well as he knows us," Lindamood wrote in her January 1993 *Automobile* road test, "you don't need to be driving a Z28."

Lindamood described the new Z28 as "a car designed and engineered to get you in trouble," which it most certainly was. When *Car and Driver* compared a 1993 Z28 to a Mustang Cobra and a Firebird Formula for its February 1993 issue, the Camaro stomped the competition. It dominated all the performance tests, with a 0-to-60 time of 5.3 seconds, a 0-to-130 time of 27.2 seconds, 70-to-0 braking distance of 165 feet, and it generated a Corvette-like 0.92g on the skid pad. It pimp-slapped the Mustang at

Above: The elongated nose was shaped as much in a wind tunnel as on a drafting table. Side vents were functional; Callaway does not design his vehicles with faux scoops, vents, or spoilers.

Opposite: Released in 1993, the Callaway Camaro C8 featured cosmetic and mechanical modifications that resulted in a rare, fast Grand Touring vehicle. This was the prototype automobile; notice the collected rain in the driver-side headlight assembly due to a faulty seal. This is the reason for prototype cars—to work the bugs out.

Designer Paul Deutschaman penned the 1993 Callaway Camaro C8, using the basic shell of the Camaro as a starting point. The long nose made entry into steep driveways a challenge.

the drag strip, covering the quarter-mile in 14 seconds flat—0.2 second faster than the magazine recorded with the legendary LT1-powered 1970 Z28—versus the Ford's 14.3-second time, and absolutely humiliated the Mustang on a road course, beating the Cobra by nearly 2 full seconds. And the Camaro did all this while still averaging 20 miles per gallon for the test.

The Camaro won the shootout by a good margin, but perhaps the highest praise for the car came in a sidebar written by *Car and Driver* Editor Patrick Bedard, who, after waxing nostalgic over the cars of the 1960s and early 1970s, compared the Camaro favorably to his all-time favorite American test car, a 1970 Pontiac Trans Am ringer prepped by legendary Pontiac ad man and subversive hot rodder Jim Wangers.

By making the rear bumper cover flush with the rear light assembly, the Callaway Camaro C8 improved aerodynamics and created a visually smoother appearance.

Yet Another Pace Car

For the buyer looking for a subdued high-performance Camaro, Chevrolet offered RPO B4C. Conversely, the division offered RPO B5A—a $995 Indianapolis 500 pace car replica—for buyers seeking anything but subdued. In 1993, for the fourth time in its history, the Camaro was selected to pace the Indianapolis 500, and once again Chevrolet capitalized on the honor with a special-edition car for customers. Chevrolet General Manager Jim Perkins, who had just returned to the GM fold after a stint at Toyota (where he helped launch the Japanese firm's Lexus brand), drove the pace car that year.

Chevrolet built the pace car replica in extremely limited quantities, perhaps in part because the graphic treatment wasn't everyone's cup of tea. The basic black-over-white paint was striking, but the maroon, lavender, yellow, and baby-blue ribbon stripes that festoon the car inside and out were definitely an acquired taste: acquired by just 633 Camaro buyers, to be precise. That low number was the result of an all-new assembly plant ramping up production of an all-new car that required a complex two-tone paint job in an all-new paint shop.

Chevrolet ramped up production slowly, building just 39,103 Camaros for the 1993 model year. Perkins wanted to avoid the quality-control issues experienced when

Buyers of the 1993 Callaway Camaro C8 enjoyed a bit more power than the stock Camaro. The 6.3-liter V-8 was rated at 404 horsepower and 412 lb-ft of torque, enough to propel the C8 to 60 miles per hour in only 4.7 seconds.

Above: While the styling of the 1993 Callaway Camaro C8 was based on the Camaro, it borrowed stylistically from other vehicles as well, including Ferrari's aluminum grill.

Opposite: With 404 horsepower beneath the long hood, the Callaway Camaro C8 could cover the quarter-mile in 13.1 seconds at 110 miles per hour and had a top speed of 172 miles per hour. It could generate 0.94g on the skidpad.

Chevrolet launched the 1982 Camaro, so the division took a cautious approach to production, addressing every minor issue as it cropped up. *Automobile*'s Jean Lindamood summed up the reputation the third-generation Camaro had developed when she wrote: "Chevrolet is really asking for a big leap of faith. It's asking you to believe that this brawny, 3,373-pound two-plus-two won't shake itself to smithereens."

Chevrolet may have been asking a lot of buyers, but in return it took the time to get the car right. This methodical approach worked, and the 1993 car was the least problematic Camaro ever built up until that time. When *Road & Track* did a long-term test of a 1994 Z28 convertible, the car did not have a single problem worth mentioning. When *Car and Driver* finished a 40,000-mile torture test of a 1995 Z28, that magazine's editors became true believers in the new Camaro's long-term integrity. Editor Phil Berg noted that "this Z28 barely makes a blip on our squeak-and-rattle meter." In what was perhaps an even greater sign of progress, the magazine averaged 22 miles per gallon over 40,000 miles from a car capable of running the quarter-mile in 14 seconds and topping out at 155 miles per hour.

Previous page: Like most concept vehicles, the California Design Camaro deliberately went over the top, wearing flowing lines and dramatic angles. And like most concept vehicles, design elements would make it onto production cars.

Below: While an aggressive nose like this would be untenable on a production car, concept vehicles, by their very nature, allow stylists to pen designs that are full of attitude.

Chevrolet's dedication to quality kept Camaro sales artificially low for the 1993 model year, but even if production had proceeded at top speed, it is unlikely that the car would have sold in huge numbers. The years 1992 and 1993 were terrible years for the U.S. auto industry. Competition was fierce—Japanese cars took a larger share of the U.S. auto market every year—but the most daunting problem car makers faced was best summed up by Bill Clinton in his successful 1992 presidential campaign: "It's the economy, stupid."

Renewed Pony Car Competition

General Motors wasn't the only American automaker hit hard by the economic recession of the early 1990s; Ford, too, took a hit, selling just 114,228 Mustangs in 1993. Still, the fact that Ford sold more than two Mustangs for every Camaro Chevy sold bode poorly for the future of the Camaro, especially given that the Camaro was a brand-new car while the Mustang featured a body style that had changed very little in 15 years and that the Z28

produced 275 horsepower while the Mustang GT produced just 205 horsepower. A limited-production Cobra R version of the Mustang produced 235 horsepower, though this extremely expensive car still couldn't outrun the new Camaro.

The Camaro's future became even bleaker the following year, when Ford introduced a new Mustang. When Ford redesigned its Mustang for 1994, its designers did not follow Chevrolet's lead and adopt trendy styling. Rather than looking to Japan or Europe for inspiration, as Chevrolet had done, Ford stuck with a distinctly American look, mining the Mustang's own rich heritage and incorporating styling cues from the car's past.

Performance-wise, the Mustang fell short of the Camaro. The reskinned Mustang kept the previous car's wartlike Fox chassis as well as the 5-liter engine, now producing 215 horsepower, making it no match for the Camaro's refined chassis and powerful 5.7-liter LT1. *Hot Rod* compared the Mustang and the Camaro in its August 1994 issue and said the Camaro's bigger engine "makes the around-town, stoplight grand prix a Camaro show." The Camaro regularly beat the Mustang in comparison tests, but the

Looking fresh from a science-fiction film, the tight interior of the California Design Camaro displayed little that would see production, but as eye-candy, the public ate it up.

Mustang looked right, and it looked American. Production at the Sainte Therese plant ramped up, and Chevrolet produced a respectable 119,799 Camaros for the 1994 model year. But Ford sold 123,598 Mustangs that year, which was a bit disheartening, considering how much better the Camaro performed.

In 1994, Chevrolet reintroduced the convertible version of the Camaro. The year-long delay had been necessitated by the need to keep the new convertible free of the foibles that had haunted the previous version. Rod Michaelson, GM's assistant segment manager for sporty cars, told *Car and Driver*'s John Phillips: "Jim Perkins told me, 'Screw it—introduce the convertible when it's defect free.' " Perkins had learned the value of building a quality car from his work with Lexus, and he put that knowledge to good use with the fourth-generation Camaro. Michaelson spent the additional year of development time well, engineering in all the extra bracing and structural work the convertible would need to be rigid enough to avoid the shakes, rattles, and squeaks of the previous convertibles.

For the Camaro's 30th anniversary, Chevrolet supplied the Indianapolis Motor Speedway with a pace car for the Brickyard 400 NASCAR stock car race. The public could, as in years before, buy street-legal versions of the vehicle, every one Artic White with Hugger Orange stripes. *General Motors Corp. Used with permission, GM Media Archives*

Opposite: In the early 1990s, the California Design Camaro was wowing auto show crowds with its dramatic

Chevrolet reprised the simple, vivid, and unmistakable paint scheme of the 1969 Camaro Indy pace car for its 1997 iteration. *General Motors Corp. Used with permission, GM Media Archives*

The new convertible provided a much more inviting space for its occupants than did the previous model. The rear window was glass instead of plastic and featured an electric defroster, the power top went up and down with the push of a button, sealed tightly against the windshield, and, when up, a cloth lining covered the formerly exposed struts and braces. *Car and Driver* called it "the most convenient convertible we have tested since the Mercedes 500SL. And it is almost as pretty." The convertible gained 153 pounds over the coupe, and it lost over a half-second in quarter-mile performance, but as *Car and Driver* editor Andre Idzikowski noted, "The *raison d'etre* of this car is open-air motoring, and it does that superbly."

Chevrolet made a couple of transmission changes that year, one good and one bad. The good: Chevrolet switched the optional automatic transmission to a much-improved

This impressive photograph shows the history of the Camaro at the Indianapolis Motor Speedway circa 1997. Only the Corvette has paced the Indianapolis 500 more times. *General Motors Corp. Used with permission, GM Media Archives*

computerized unit, which helped bump EPA gas-mileage estimates up to 17/26 city/highway miles per gallon for the Z28 and 19/28 for the Sport Coupe. The bad: in 1994, Chevrolet introduced a horrible device that directed the gearshift lever from first to fourth under light acceleration. In theory, this system made the car more fuel efficient, but *Car and Driver* noted: "It has on us the opposite effect, provoking jackrabbit starts." Fortunately, this misguided feature could be disabled by "cutting the green wire," as one Chevrolet engineer explained.

Otherwise, Chevrolet's Camaro team barely made a change to the car in its sophomore year. It didn't have to—the car was that good. Chevrolet made even fewer changes to the Z28 in 1995 but made Buick's 200-horsepower 3.8-liter V-6 available as a $350 option on the Sport Coupe. (It became the standard base engine the following year.) This swap addressed one of the few complaints about the Camaro Sport Coupe, namely an underpowered V-6 engine that *Road & Track* described as "Casper Milquetoast in a macho wrapper." Sales rose slightly, to 122,738 units, in part reflecting an improving U.S. economy. Sales improved at an even faster rate for the Mustang, with Ford selling 165,037 units for the 1995 model year.

In an effort to improve the weight distribution, Chevrolet engineers moved the engine in the fourth generation as far aft as possible. The back half of the engine fit underneath the base of the windshield.

Sports Car International compared the two most exclusive, high-performance versions of the Mustang and Camaro—the Cobra R and the 1LE, respectively—for the magazine's July 1995 issue. The Cobra R was a limited-production street racer produced by Ford's Special Vehicles Team (SVT), formed from the remains of the earlier Special Vehicle Operations (SVO) crew. Like the 1LE, the Cobra R was a racing platform stripped of all power-robbing, heavy luxury items, like air conditioning, sound insulation, radio, rear seats, and power windows and door locks. The SVT folks massaged Ford's 5.8-liter (that's 351 Windsor, in American) to produce 300 horsepower and 365 lb-ft of torque, then stuffed it into the stripped-down Mustang coupe. Between the cost of paying for SVT's development work, having Roush Technologies install the engines, and compensating the EPA for the car's gas-guzzler tax, the list price of the Cobra R worked out to $37,599. Buyers had to promise that they would only use the 250 cars Ford built for racing competition and not license them as street cars, though they were legally free to license them.

By the time the fourth-generation Camaro came out, building pace car replicas had become a tradition. It made sense to celebrate the 30th Anniversary of the Camaro in 1997 with a pace car replica. Embroidered seats were part of the celebratory package.

Buyers of the 1LE simply had to check the right option code on the order sheet, plunk down $18,160, and drive away with a factory race car. The Camaro produced 25 fewer horsepower and 40 lb-ft less torque, but even so, both cars turned in nearly identical performance, with 14.1-second quarter-mile times and skid pad numbers of 0.90g. The Mustang beat the Camaro in 0-to-60 times—5.4 seconds versus 5.5 seconds—but the Camaro had more top-end speed—155 miles per hour versus 151 miles per hour—a faster average slalom speed—66 miles per hour versus 65 miles per hour—and shorter braking distances.

The Camaro won the magazine's comparison test outright, without even factoring in the price. The price difference of almost $20,000 put into perspective what an incredible performance bargain the Camaro was, yet the Mustang continued to outperform the Camaro in the one contest that mattered most: attracting buyers.

For 1996, Ford introduced a new engine for the Mustang, a 4.6-liter V-8 that abandoned traditional pushrods for overhead cams. Initially, the engine produced the same 215 horsepower as the aging 5-liter it replaced. It was still no match for the LT1 engine that came as standard equipment in the Z28, now producing 285 horsepower, thanks to a new dual-exhaust system with advanced computer controls. Ford again produced a high-buck Cobra version featuring a double-overhead-cam 32-valve version of the new 4.6-liter engine that produced 305 horsepower, but Chevrolet had its own limited-edition Camaro capable of taking on the Cobra.

Nothing says "Camaro" like white paint with Hugger Orange stripes. Regular production option Z4C bought the special paint, trim, and either leather or white leather with black-and-white hound's-tooth upholstery.

Street Legal Performance

In 1986, a far-sighted fellow named Ed Hamburger started a company that developed automotive aftermarket parts to improve performance while still meeting emissions standards, called, appropriately, Street Legal Performance (SLP). The company's first collaboration with an automaker occurred in 1992, when SLP and Pontiac worked together to produce the Firebird Firehawk SLP, a version of the Trans Am that produced 350 horsepower and 390 lb-ft of torque, thanks in part to an SLP-designed Ram-Air fresh air intake. This 13-second quarter-mile terror was a true muscle car, though a very expensive one at $40,000.

In 1996, SLP worked with Chevrolet to bring back an iconic name to the Camaro lineup: SS. Beginning that year, Chevrolet shipped Z28s to SLP's facility in Quebec. Once there, SLP produced a Camaro SS that, like the Firehawk, used a forced-air

Functional fog lamps, front fascia, headlights, hood, and fenders were new for the 1998 Z28. List price of the four-seat sports car was $20,995, and 17,573 were built.

Thanks to a 305-horsepower version of the Corvette's V-8, the 1998 Camaro Z28 had no problem blurring the scenery. Z28s came with black roofs, while the base Camaros wore body-color tops.

By 1998, Camaro interiors had assumed a more organic look, with soft-touch materials and flowing lines. But make no mistake—the rear seats were only fit for groceries and kids.

induction system and a few other traditional hot-rodding techniques to generate 305 horsepower from the 5.7-liter engine, dubbed "R7T" when used in the Camaro SS. Torque remained the same as with the LT1, at 325 lb-ft. The modified engine, along with 17-inch wheels, sticky race tires, aerodynamic bodywork, and a lightly modified rear suspension added $3,999 to the Z28's $19,390 base price. From there, a buyer could add other handling and performance options, like a Hurst shifter and a freer-flowing exhaust system that bumped power output by another 5 horsepower. The as-tested price of the SS *Car and Driver* tested for its October 1995 issue came to $28,770 when all the extra amenities were tabulated, but for that price, a buyer got a hand-built 154-mile-per-hour supercar that was "nicely sorted, rattle-free, and comfortable." Even at that price, SLP's Camaro SS was a bargain compared to Ford's Cobra.

Car and Driver generated the fastest quarter-mile time it had ever achieved in a Camaro with the SS: 13.7 seconds. *Sports Car International* turned in an even more impressive performance: a 13.3-second quarter-mile and a top speed of 159 miles per hour.

The Camaro kept getting better, but the Mustang still outsold the Camaro in 1996, 107,891 units versus 61,362 units, including the 2,410 Camaro SS models built by SLP. In an attempt to attract a broader audience, Chevrolet resurrected the RS model in both coupe and convertible form. As before, the RS combined sporty, Z28-like styling with the mechanicals from the base Sport Coupe, but the model proved a slow seller, with Chevy dealers moving just 11,085 RS models in 1996.

Chromed, five-spoke wheels were part of the Z28 package for 1998. Bright Red, paint code 81, was the most popular color that year, with a total of 11,734 units covered in this ticket-attracting hue.

Camaro 30 Years

In 1997, Chevrolet celebrated the 30th anniversary of the Camaro with RPO Z4C, a commemorative pace car edition. Unlike past pace car replicas, this one didn't commemorate the Indianapolis 500, but rather the Brickyard 400, a stock car race held at the Indianapolis

In an attempt to reduce the potential for vapor-lock issues, the factory wrapped the fuel lines with foil to reflect engine compartment heat.

Chevrolet stylists beautifully integrated the functional spoiler into the rear hatch on the fourth-generation Camaro. The badging on the 1998 Camaro Z28 was not subtle.

Motor Speedway each year, a nod to the growing popularity of NASCAR racing in the United States. Chevrolet revived the Arctic-White-with-Hugger-Orange paint scheme of the 1969 Indy 500 pace car for the Brickyard replica and even recreated the original's hound's-tooth interior. Apparently, customers found this replica more aesthetically appealing than the 1993 car; 4,533 buyers opted for the $575 RPO Z4C package.

The 1998 Z28's length was 9 inches longer than the original 1967 Camaro, yet the wheelbase was 2 inches shorter. Both front and rear overhangs were considerable.

Chevrolet teamed up with SLP to produce another Camaro SS in 1997. That year, SLP built 3,137 SS models that once again added $3,999 to the Z28's base price, which had grown to $20,115. Of those cars, a small number contained a very special engine: the LT4. In 1996, Chevrolet had developed this hot-rodded version of the LT1 engine, which produced 330 horsepower and 340 lb-ft of torque, for the last year of fourth-generation Corvette production. SLP balanced and blueprinted each LT4 it received from Chevrolet and mounted 106 of them in Camaro SS models, making these cars as rare as they are fast.

All of this wasn't enough to revive the Camaro's sinking sales, which fell to 60,202 for the 1997 model year. Mustang sales also fell, but Ford still sold 100,304 Mustangs for the year, a fairly healthy number compared to Camaro sales.

Dual halogen lamps in the headlight cluster provided plenty of illumination, while the near-flush design improved aerodynamics.

Opposite: A brute in svelte clothing, the 2000 SS could accelerate to 60 miles per hour in just 5.5 seconds and dash the length of the quarter-mile in 13.9 seconds. Having a 5.7-liter, 320-horsepower V-8 might have had something to do with it.

For 2000, the Camaro wore its largest wheels ever—cast-aluminum 17-inchers shod with Goodyear F1 GS radials that allowed the SS model to stick to corners like a hungry leach.

An American Lexus

When Jim Perkins left Toyota to take the reigns of the Chevrolet Division, he brought with him a single-minded devotion to quality that helped make the fourth-generation Camaro one of the best-built cars Chevrolet had produced since the 1960s. He also brought with him a taste for the looks of sporty Japanese coupes like the Lexus SC400, a taste reflected in the lines and proportions of the Camaro. In 1998, Chevrolet took the look of the

Camaro even closer to that of the Lexus. Flush headlights replaced the sunken headlights of the 1993–1997 cars. The new lights may or may not have been more aerodynamic, but they did a better job lighting up the road than did the older, sunken units.

The price paid was that the new face looked more like a Japanese sport coupe and even less like an American muscle car. To make the car look more aggressive, Chevrolet stylists added some curves to the flat, sloping fourth-generation hood, complementing

In the center of the hood is a functional hood scoop, drawing cool outside air into the induction system. All of the engine's cooling air was fed from underneath the front air dam.

For model year 2000, the SS option, RPO WU8, was a pricey buy at $3,950. Despite the cost, 8,913 customers found it in their wallets to pay up.

the shape of the new lights, and installed a larger grille opening. Chevrolet designers developed five different designs for the facelifted car and showed them to survey groups consisting not only of Camaro owners, but also of Mustang and Firebird owners, and the more aggresive designs were soundly rejected. The different face was an obvious change, but the most important change for the 1998 Z28 lurked beneath the reshaped hood: the new LS1 engine.

When mounted in the Camaro, this 5.7-liter V-8 produced the same 305 horse-power as the hot-rodded SLP LT1 engine, and produced 335 lb-ft of torque, 10 more

The Super Sport name entered Chevrolet's lexicon in 1957 with the debut of the magnesium-bodied Corvette SS. Fast-forward nearly half a century, and it still stood for performance and presence.

Berger Chevrolet in Grand Rapids, Michigan, built high-performance Camaros in the late 1960s, and as the Camaro neared the end of its production run, Berger continued to construct powerful street cars.

than the LT1. Chevrolet constructed the LS1 entirely of aluminum, making it the first all-aluminum engine available in a Camaro since the ZL-1 of 1969. Unlike the rare and expensive ZL-1, the LS1 came as standard equipment in the Z28. With its deep-skirt engine block, composite-construction intake manifold, distributorless ignition, and an oil pan that added structural rigidity to the chassis, the LS1 was the most radically new Chevrolet small-block engine since the division's first overhead-valve V-8 introduced nearly five decades earlier. *Car and Driver*, which turned a 13.8-second quarter-mile time with the revised Z28 it tested for its December 1997 issue, wrote: "This new LS1 pulls to its 6,000-rpm redline with more enthusiasm and less commotion than its iron-block predecessor, which had a 5,700-rpm redline. In sound and feel, this new engine is simply more refined."

Refined or not, the 5.7-liter engine was still engineered to get its driver in trouble. *Automobile*'s Kevin Clemens summed up the appeal of the LS1-equipped Camaro when he tested a Z28 for the magazine's November 1997 issue:

The car feels nearly bulletproof. In a morning spent abusing clutch and tires, doing smoky burnouts, the Z28 gave not a murmur of protest. And it's so easy. Switch off the traction control, slide the short-throw six-speed manual transmission into first, and give a little gas to get the car rolling. Then, any time you want, roll onto the throttle and the 235/55R-16 Goodyears can't hold back the fury of the new son of the small-block Chevy. Smoke rolls off the tires and the car jumps sideways in a heartbeat.

Chevrolet once again created an SS version of the Camaro, though now SLP played a much smaller role in the process. In 1998, Chevrolet built 3,025 Z28 SS models. Division engineers brought the output of the new LS1 up to 320 horsepower and torque up to 345 lb-ft in SS application. A new stainless-steel exhaust system deserved the bulk of the credit for the increased power. In 1998, the price of the SS fell to $3,500, a saving that was more than offset by the rise of the Z28's base price to $20,995.

While the performance news regarding the 1998 Camaro was all good, the sales results weren't so good; Chevy dealers moved just 54,026 Camaros for the model year. Meanwhile, Mustang sales jumped to 170,642. Ford was selling three Mustangs for every Camaro Chevrolet sold, despite the fact that the Camaro handled much better and cranked out 80 more horsepower than the aging Ford.

Above: Essentially stock, the interior of a Berger Camaro is a comfortable place to be. Dual air bags were standard.

Opposite: Most of the modifications on a Berger Camaro are under the skin, like a 375-horsepower V-8 and a trick exhaust system.

With 375 horsepower and a 3.73:1 rear axle ratio, the Berger Camaro could hustle down the road better than most cars. Berger Camaros have always seen very limited production.

A Retro Restyle for the Mustang

The Camaro continued to beat the Mustang in magazine test after magazine test. *Car and Driver* compared a Z28 to a Mustang GT in February 1999, and the Camaro won every speed contest, every handling contest, and every comfort and convenience contest. It even turned in better average gas mileage—22 miles per gallon versus the Mustang's 20 miles per gallon. When *Road & Track* compared an SVT Mustang Cobra to a Camaro Z28 SS in April 1999, the less-expensive Camaro again turned in better performance numbers than the Mustang. When *Car and Driver* tested the 2000-model-year versions of a Z28 SS against an SVT Cobra and a Firebird Trans Am in August 1999, once again the Camaro won all the marbles.

Opposite: In a nod to past Camaros, the Berger Camaros wear heritage stripes, updated to flow around the functional cold-air induction scoop on the hood.

The tonneau cover on the Berger Camaro is stock Camaro, meaning it's a three-piece unit. It takes a bit of effort to get it on, but it maintains the sleek lines and does not flutter in the wind.

The Camaro would beat more than its rival pony cars; when equipped with the 1LE package, a Camaro SS would soundly trounce the hottest Corvette of the period, the Z51. Unfortunately Chevrolet marketers were not allowed to publicize this fact because GM feared it would dampen Corvette sales.

Clearly buyers weren't choosing the Mustang over the Camaro for any empirical reasons easily measured on a performance chart or spec sheet. Customers were putting their money where their hearts were. The Mustang's retro styling cues were enough to trigger the buy impulse in customers and get them to sign the loan papers and drive new Mustangs off dealer lots. The Camaro was handsome enough, but it used a subtle, inoffensive design language that didn't speak to buyers. The styling cues of the Mustang spoke to three times as many customers as did the styling of the Camaro.

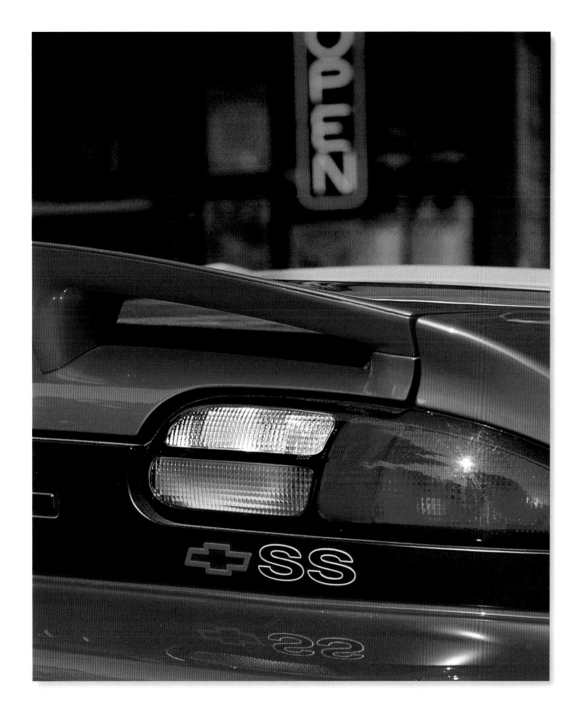

Ford got the message buyers were sending loud and clear, and for 1999 it introduced a redesigned Mustang that was even more retro, looking almost like something Steve McQueen would have driven, had he still been alive. The Mustang GT's power output rose to 260 horsepower. This still wasn't enough to run with the Camaro, and the ancient Fox chassis was getting to be an embarrassment. These factors dampened the car's appeal to serious hot-rodders, but the retro style made up most of the difference, and the Mustang still outsold the Camaro by a nearly three-to-one margin, with Ford selling 126,067 Mustangs to Chevrolet's 42,098 Camaros.

Next page: For drivers having difficulty merging onto freeways, Berger Chevrolet would sell you a 2002 Camaro ZL-1. With 600 horsepower under the hood, the biggest problem was getting the rear tires to stop spinning and grip the road.

The big number on the fender of the 2002 Berger ZL-1 wasn't for show, but it tended to dissuade other drivers from looking for a race. This is the only Berger ZL-1 in this color.

A Judas' Kiss

Chevrolet seemed to be in a holding pattern with the Camaro. Inside the company, those who wanted to kill the F-body program had gained the upper hand, and Chevrolet made virtually no changes for the Camaro's final four years of production. Changes were limited to suspension upgrades and breathing improvements to the SS models, and these changes were driven by SLP owner Ed Hamburger and his chieft engineer, Jeff Yachnin. In 2001, Chevrolet bumped horsepower and torque of the LS1 to 310 and 340 lb-ft, respectively. To keep pace, SS power jumped to 325 horsepower and 350 lb-ft of torque. In 2002, Chevrolet offered a 35th anniversary edition of the SS with funky checkered-flag graphics on the hood and trunk lid, but it was something of a Judas' kiss for the iconic Camaro—Chevrolet had made the decision to pull the plug on the nameplate, and 2002 was the last year for Camaro production.

The sales numbers had remained grim. In 2000, they rose slightly to 45,461 units, but then plummeted to 29,009 units in 2001, the worst year ever for Camaro sales. In 2002, they rose back up to 41,776 units, but most of that was because everyone knew the end was coming and many Camaro fans wanted to snap up the last of the breed. Because of this, Chevrolet shortened the produciton year for the 2001 model, knowing many buyers would prefer to wait until the final 2002 model went into production.

In fact, the decision to kill the car had been finalized in 1996, so very little development money had been alloted to the F-body program. Chevrolet wisely invested what money was available on improving performance; if these were to be the last of the

Heavy Metal, version 2002. Berger Chevrolet sold a limited number of these 600-horsepower street-legal beasts. Like the original ZL-1 from 1969, the newer engine was all aluminum.

Camaros, they damned sure were going to the the fastest. Because the decision had been made to end F-body prodcution, GM ceased replacing workers at the Ste. Theresa production facility. By 2002 the plant had lost so many workers through attrition that it couldn't fill all its orders for 2002-models F cars.

One bright spot during those final grim years had been steadily rising sales of the expensive-but-potent SS. In 1999, 4,829 buyers bought SS models. In 2000, that number rose to 8,913 buyers. In 2001, only 6,332 buyers bought the SS, but that number represented nearly 22 percent of all 2001 Camaro buyers. In 2002, 11,191 Camaro buyers spent an additional $3,625 to SS-ize their Z28s, and 3,369 of those buyers spent another $2,500 to get the 35th anniversary edition of the Z28 SS. The car would have died much earlier—the initial plan was to kill the Camaro after 1997—but the popularity of the LS1-powered cars kept the Camaro in the lineup until September 1, 2002, when the Camaro no longer complied with federal head-impact standards.

In 2003, the Camaro was gone from Chevrolet's lineup, leaving only the expensive Corvette sports car and the front-wheel-drive Monte Carlo SS for performance enthusiasts who wanted a bowtie on their car. That seemed to be the end of the Camaro story, but with the SS anniversary edition, at least the car went out on a high note.

Above: In the not-so-subtle category is the 2002 Berger ZL-1 Camaro. This particular car featured special-order paint and gold-leaf trim. In case someone fails to understand the car's unique character, 600 horsepower soon set things right.

Right: Berger Chevrolet in Grand Rapids, Michigan, teamed up with *Hot Rod* Magazine to build 37 Hot Rod Edition Camaros. Not all were in this subtle red finish.

Starting with a 5.7-liter V-8, Berger Chevrolet coaxed 380 horsepower from the small-block installed in the Hot Rod Edition Camaro. The factory warranty remained intact.

The huge black area in the front of the Berger/Hot Rod Edition Camaro just looks like the grille. In fact, it passes no air at all, but the SS badge looks great there.

Special embroidery in the back of the seats in the 2002 Berger/Hot Rod Edition made sure that occupants didn't forget just what they were riding in. A healthy 380-horse engine meant the speedometer needle could touch the stupid numbers.

Berger Chevrolet installed its engine output callouts on the forward end of the front fenders of its Hot Rod Edition. These were honest horses, not marketing Shetlands.

EPILOGUE
The Resurrected Camaro

The Camaro's death in the early years of the twenty-first century seemed logical. No nameplate lives forever. When the F-bodies died, they joined such fabled cars in muscle car heaven as Chevrolet's Chevelle, Pontiac's GTO, Buick's Grand Sport, Dodge's Challenger and Charger, Plymouth's 'Cuda and Road Runner, Oldsmobile's 4-4-2, and even the Plymouth and Oldsmobile brands themselves. Young drivers lusted for fast and furious sport compacts like Subaru's WRX and Mitsubishi's Evo; muscle cars were what their weird uncles drove.

One car bucked that trend: Ford's Mustang. While Camaro sales withered and the car died of neglect, Ford continued to put lipstick on the old piglike Fox-based car, and people of all ages continued to buy it. About the same time GM decided to kill off the

Chevrolet pulled no small amount of styling cues from the iconic 1969 Camaro to infuse the Camaro concept car with the muscular aggressiveness of the original. Built on the corporation's Zeta architecture, it will share underpinnings with other General Motors vehicles, including the Pontiac G8 sedan. *General Motors Corp. Used with permission, GM Media Archives*

It's 1969 again. The latest production Camaro may not be as show-car flashy as this concept, but it will incorporate lots of styling cues from the first-generation Camaros. Note the gauge cluster in front of the center console-mounted shifter and the large circular gauges in the instrument panel. *General Motors Corp. Used with permission, GM Media Archives*

F-body program, Ford began developing the first all-new Mustang in over a quarter-century. In the fall of 2004, Ford introduced the fastest, best-handling Mustang ever. Based on the Lincoln LS platform, the most sophisticated rear-wheel-drive chassis in Ford's lineup, the new Mustang is a true muscle car. The current version of the OHC aluminum 4.6-liter powerplant produces 300 horsepower and 320 lb-ft of torque, enough to propel the 3,600-pound Mustang through the quarter-mile in the high 13-second range.

Ford used the Lincoln LS platform as a jumping-off point for developing the new Mustang. The LS platform used a sophisticated independent rear suspension, but the Mustang featured an old-fashion live-axle design. Initially, the press squawked about this cost-saving measure, at least until they drove the new car. The drawbacks of the live axle make themselves known if the Mustang encounters rough pavement in a hard corner—sharp bumps on a freeway ramp will make the back end step out of line—but the design has the some advantages, too. Live axles are especially effective when it comes to twisting 320 lb-ft of torque into the pavement on a hard drag strip launch.

It's easy to think that you're in a 1969 Camaro looking at the center console of the Camaro concept. The cluster of ancillary engine gauges forward of the beefy shifter is pure 1969. *General Motors Corp. Used with permission, GM Media Archives*

The live-axle design is inexpensive to design and produce, too, helping keep the base price of the Mustang GT down around $25,000.

Perhaps most important for the intended market, the new Mustang looked right. Ford captured the perfect combination of Mustang styling cues and modern proportions to create a car that made people stop what they were doing and stare as it drove past them. The Mustang had been trading on its retro good looks for a generation, and that was enough to put Chevrolet's Camaro out of business. Now it had even better looks and had the performance to back up its appearance. The public responded, and

The current-generation Mustang has had the pony car field to itself for quite a few years, and with the introduction of the 500-horsepower GT500, it has established itself as the car to beat. The 2009 Camaro will offer powerplants strong enough to challenge the entire Mustang line.

The Camaro concept displays the long hood/short deck proportions that made the first-generation Camaro a success. The faux vents in front of the rear wheels pay homage to the 1969 model. *General Motors Corp. Used with permission, GM Media Archives*

the new Mustang was a hit. Calendar-year sales jumped from 129,858 Mustangs in 2004 to 160,975 in 2005, making the car the only bright spot in what was otherwise a very bad year for Ford Motor Company.

The Second Coming—and Going—of the Goat

Ford's Mustang proved that there was still a viable market for a muscular rear-wheel-drive sport coupe, one that General Motors should not ignore. But the situation at GM was radically different than it had been four decades earlier, when Chevrolet Division only had to raid its parts bin to create the Camaro. This time around, the only rear-wheel-drive platform in Chevrolet's automotive stable was the exotic and expensive-to-produce Corvette sports car. Chevrolet sold several front-wheel-drive performance cars, but such cars are not and never will be muscle cars. Even when you stuff a V-8 engine in a front-wheel-drive car, as Pontiac had done with its Grand Prix, it is not a muscle car. A muscle car needs to generate billowing plumes of smoke from the back tires; when those plumes come from the front of the car, it just looks as if something has broken inside the engine.

Pontiac Division had addressed this problem by raiding the stable of Holden, General Motors' Australian subsidiary. Holden built the Monaro, a great potential muscle car. In addition to delivering power to the back tires, the Monaro already had a true muscle car engine: the Corvette's LT1. In Monaro trim, the 5.7-liter engine produced 350 horsepower.

Unfortunately, the Monaro looked like a two-door coupe version of a mid-1990s Ford Taurus. Pontiac was given a limited budget for converting the Monaro into a GTO, and most of that money was spent moving the steering wheel from the right side of the car to the left, leaving very little capital for any restyling effort. Other changes needed to homologate the car for sale in the U.S. market added futher cost. For example, relocating the fuel tank cost over $20 million. Pontiac added some GTO badges and a Pontiac-style front-end treatment and brought the car to the U.S. market in 2004. The 2004 GTO was a solid performer, but the car's appearance was nondescript at best. Even though the car was quick and handled better than any previous GTO, Pontiac sold just 13,569 GTOs in the 2004 calendar year.

In 2005, Pontiac designers made a few token efforts at giving the GTO more presence, like punching a couple of Ram Air-style holes in the hood and bolting a Judge-like wing to

Next page: The Chevrolet product lineup will include a coupe and convertible Camaro. Ford's Mustang, the Camaro's traditional rival, will no longer be playing in a field of one. *General Motors Corp. Used with permission, GM Media Archives*

the rear deck, but there was only so much they could do with a car that looked like a well-worn bar of soap.

Pontiac also borrowed the new LS2 engine from the recently released C6 version of the Corvette and stuck it in the GTO. With this 6-liter, pushrod, two-valve-per-cylinder small-block V-8 that produced 400 horsepower and 400 lb-ft of torque, the GTO now had a great engine to match its chassis. The 3,800-pound car became a genuine 13-second-quarter-mile muscle car.

Just as the Camaro had spanked the Mustang in performance tests throughout the 1990s, the new GTO outperformed the new Mustang every time magazines pitted the two cars against one another. But by this time, even magazine editors, like the general public, tended to follow their hearts more than their heads when selecting a winning car. The GTO was faster, handled better, and had a roomier, more comfortable interior, but editors universally chose the Mustang as the winner simply because they loved the look of Ford's new pony car. They just couldn't warm up to the nondescript GTO. Nor could the buying public; Pontiac sold just 11,590 GTOs in calendar year 2005 and dropped the car after the 2006 model year.

General Motors' director of exterior design for rear-wheel-drive and performance vehicles, Tom Peters, pointed out that the primary difference between the coupe and convertible Camaro is in the rear fenders and trunk lid. The production Camaro will have a taller windshield but for the most part will appear much like the concept. *General Motors Corp. Used with permission, GM Media Archives*

Interior designers had to move the rear seats closer together to allow room for the Camaro concept's folding top mechanism. Micah Jones, creative designer for the Camaro interior, used the Audi A4 cabriolet as the design target, including a rigid tonneau top. *General Motors Corp. Used with permission, GM Media Archives*

A Designer's Car

The failure of the revived GTO might have killed GM management's enthusiasm for a new muscle car for good, had the Mustang's success not shown them that this most-American of genres still had legs in the market.

Chevrolet began working on a Camaro concept car in early 2005. The project grew out of a conversation Ed Welburn, GM vice president of global design, had with designer Bob Boniface over beers not long after Boniface took charge of Chevrolet's Advanced Design Studio. Welburn asked Boniface what he planned to build as his first project, and Boniface said he'd like to do a new Camaro. Like Boniface, Welburn was a huge Camaro fan, but he knew that such a project would meet resistance from GM management. "Just don't tell anybody," Welburn advised.

Boniface began working on a concept in April 2005. About halfway through the year, designer Tom Peters began working on the Camaro project. Peters had been the project leader for the sixth-generation Corvette. His team built a concept car using the Cadillac

STS architecture, though the plan was to base any possible production Camaro on the new Holden Zeta architecture. When the Australian Division redesigned the Zeta architecture for the next-generation Monaro, it engineered the car to be either right-hand or left-hand drive, which meant that developing versions for the North American market was a much-less-expensive proposition.

Peters' crew produced a modern car that was unmistakably a Camaro. The concept car measured 186.2 inches long, almost identical to the original Camaro, but it was 79.4 inches wide, almost 5 inches wider than the original, reflecting a more modern performance car aesthetic. With its strong lines and powerful stance, the car was a *tour de force* of automotive design. It captured the details of the iconic 1969 Camaro, such as the pointed grille and vents in front of the rear-wheel openings, in a design that was both a classical muscle car and a modern, forward-thinking performance car.

"My charge to the design team was for them to do the meanest, scrappiest, street-fighting dog they could sketch," Peters told *Road & Track*'s Matt DeLorenzo. Peters'

Oozing menace, the Camaro concept convertible will offer a six-cylinder engine as well a slate of V-8s. A high-power SS version is a given. A full-width grille with the headlights pushed to the corners evokes the essence of the first-generation Camaro. *General Motors Corp. Used with permission, GM Media Archives*

High-back, bolstered seats allude to the performance that will be built into the new Camaro. A full slate of restraint systems will be engineered into the new Camaro, including side air bags. *General Motors Corp. Used with permission, GM Media Archives*

team succeeded, producing a show car that impressed other designers as much as it impressed the press and Camaro fans.

If You Show It, You Must Build It

Perhaps the Camaro concept car impressed the fans too much. When Bob Lutz, GM's North American chairman, drove the concept onto the stage at the 2006 North American International Auto Show in Detroit on January 8, 2006, he ignited a furor among the automotive world that wouldn't subside until August 10, 2006, when GM officially

announced it would build the Camaro. In May 2006, Lutz had told *Automotive News* that Chevrolet would have to sell 100,000 Camaros per year for GM management to approve the car. Apparently, management believed that number was attainable, and Chevrolet scheduled production to begin in late 2008, with customer cars being delivered in early 2009.

In automotive terms, there is a remarkably short period between the show car's 2006 debut and the scheduled 2008 production date. Development time has been condensed in part because of the use of the existing Holden Zeta architecture. Chevrolet

While the Camaro concept uses aluminum brightwork throughout the interior, production vehicles will be able to use more cost-agreeable materials to replicate the look. *General Motors Corp. Used with permission, GM Media Archives*

In an effort to pay homage to the 1969 Camaro's red-line tires, the designers of the Camaro concept put a red line around the outside edge of the wheel. The blade-type exterior mirrors will be enlarged for the production vehicle. *General Motors Corp. Used with permission, GM Media Archives*

won't just tweak this architecture, as Pontiac had done with the GTO, but rather borrow components to create an entirely new car.

In January 2007, Chevrolet showed a convertible version of the Camaro at that year's Detroit Auto Show. This car generated even more excitement than the concept car had the previous year.

Production specifications have yet to be made public, but a six-cylinder version is likely, and the base V-8 will be the LS2 V-8. The version of the aluminum LS2 engine powering the concept car features what Chevrolet calls "Active Fuel" management, in which four cylinders are shut down under light load conditions. This means that the 400-horsepower engine can return 30 or more miles per gallon when driven with a light right foot. Driven with less restraint, the engine will make the new Camaro the fastest one ever—unless Chevrolet offers even more powerful versions.

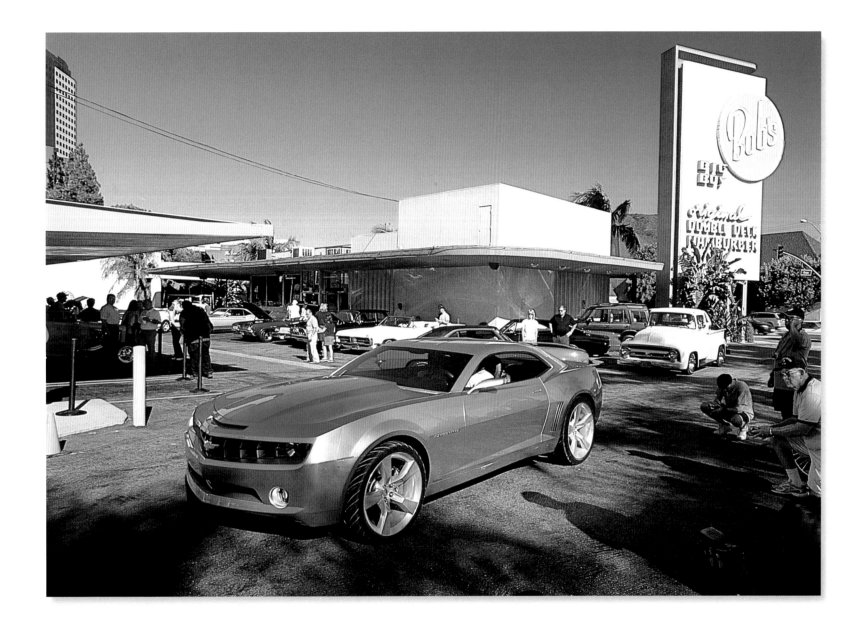

Optional engines could include a version of the aluminum 7-liter (that's 427 cubic inches, for any ZL-1 fans) LS7 engine from the Corvette Z06, which seems a logical choice for any high-end Camaro. In the Corvette, this engine produces 500 horsepower and 475 lb-ft of torque. This much power would make the top Camaro a match for Ford's Shelby Mustang Cobra GT500, which generates 500 horsepower and 480 lb-ft of torque from its supercharged 5.4-liter engine. Chevrolet may decide the Camaro has to produce less power than the Corvette and detune the LS7, but hopefully this won't happen. Historically the Camaro and the Corvette have had very distinct customer bases and have not cannibalized sales from one another.

Regardless of what happens, the new Camaro will be the most exciting car Chevrolet has produced since the debut of the original version in the fall of 1966. For Camaro fans, the best is yet to come.

In an effort to gauge public reaction to the Camaro concept, Chevrolet asked comedian Jay Leno to drive the car to the famous Friday night cruise night at the Toluca Lake Bob's Big Boy restaurant. The reaction was, well, enthusiastic.

INDEX